a language of soul.

Prince Edward Island, Canada

Library and Archives Canada
ISBN Title: *"When you get better, can you build a snowman with me?" A 'Deep Well' Perspective
for Healing in Depression: Introducing 7 Action Steps to Overcoming Depressive Symptoms.*

ISBN 978-1-7752593-0-5

www.stigmacrush.com

A 'Deep Well' Perspective for Healing in Depression

CONTENTS

ACKNOWLEDGEMENTS

In my darkest hour, you were there for me, and for this, I am forever grateful. You know who you are.

To my editor friends who graciously gave their time to review my first draft: Thank You! You'll never know how much it means to me.

Dedicated to the memory of my Dad: though I wish I would have done more for you, rest knowing that your inspiration is going to help people.

My family, I am blessed beyond words.

INTRODUCTION

Thank you for your interest in my book. Obviously, I don't know your reason for picking this up or displaying it on your screen, but you have your reason. Perhaps it's out of simple curiosity – an interest in learning a different perspective about this mental illness called depression. Or perhaps it's the other extreme: you're suffering terribly and are in that dangerous place contemplating unthinkable ways to make the hurting stop. I don't know. But whatever the reason, I'm glad you have it.

I'm glad because I sincerely believe that the information I share in this book – the perspectives, learned principles, and action steps – can have a profound and positive impact on your mental well-being. I know this because this is the same information that I leveraged to successfully heal in depression and overcome its debilitating symptoms.

The foremost intention of this book is getting the message of hope in the hands of individuals who are suffering with depression. Prior to crushing my own stigma toward this disorder, I kept my manuscript hidden under lock and key, waiting for that 'right time' to present itself so I could step up and do my part to make a difference. While I sat, I learned about friends, family members and individuals in my community struggling with their mental health; and became disturbed by tragic news stories about suicides. This made it increasingly difficult for me to keep waiting – to keep doing nothing. It made me sick to my stomach. I realized that the 'right time' was never going to come.

No matter where you are in your suffering, and no matter how hopeless you perceive things to be in your life, don't give up. You are reading this because I fought for my mental freedom, choosing not to give in to the debilitating symptoms of my disorder. I crushed my stigma completely and now I want to do my part to help you heal. I am not an aspiring writer, nor do I have ambitions to win an award for my writing. Rather, I am an individual who suffered with a mental illness and found a pathway to healing which I have documented and feel I need to share with the world. This is my purpose.

I am under no illusion: my work, this book, is not intended to cure your depression; but rather, it is to equip you with what I would consider is the single most important element you can leverage to successfully heal in this disorder: *hope*. I believe this because you and I know all too well that depression is a catalyst for hopelessness.

There is hope, always.
Jamie Dooks

This is my story…

I had just returned home from work one February evening in 2012. I pulled into the driveway and parked the car. It was about five o'clock, nearly pitch dark outside. I turned off the lights and sat back into my seat and sighed. My heart was heavy and I was anxious. I rubbed my eyes and wiped away the tear marks that stretched down the length of my face. It was an effort to remove any evidence of grief from my wife and children before walking into the house.

Crying while alone in the car was nothing new for me. In fact, it was a common occurrence that spanned over the many months leading up to this very evening. Overwhelmed by the stresses and anxieties I felt were mounting in my life, I would cry on my way to work in the morning and would cry on the way home in the evening. Sometimes I would break down for no apparent reason. I perceived a tremendous weight in my heart, so much so that I felt like I would collapse under the pressure. I felt trapped and found it difficult to breathe at times. I felt hopeless. These feelings that seeped from the perceived pressures in my life affected every aspect of my daily living.

At work, I would at times retreat to the bathroom and lock myself in the stall to conceal the emotional turmoil building up inside me. Or I would be at my desk, staring blankly at my computer screen when a sudden panic attack would force me to retreat to my car and drive away, to anywhere I could be alone. I often drove to beaches where, in the winter, I would sit on an undisturbed dock, or in the summer, track through the sand far enough away from people so I couldn't hear voices. At home, I would purposely avoid answering the telephone, or if we had company, I would routinely retreat to my room or basement for a momentary escape from the clashing sounds of voices, television sets, and banging of pots and pans. I grew sensitive to noise and was uncomfortable around crowds. It seemed that whatever the circumstance in my life, a force pulled me in the same direction: toward *isolation*. I felt like I needed to be alone. And when I was alone, I would only think about that single contemplation: *how to make the hurting stop*.

I took a deep breath and stepped out of the car and made my way into the house. As much as I tried to hide my emotions from my family, the truth of the matter was, they knew there was something wrong. Unfortunately, I was blinded to how my behavior was affecting them. I didn't recognize how the lowness in my voice, the shortness of my breath, and my brief one-worded responses, hindered attempts by my family to communicate with me. I failed to acknowledge the lack of interest I was showing in my wife and children because I found it difficult to concentrate on them. I couldn't see the neglect they were feeling every time I looked for an excuse to retreat to my bedroom to be alone. I didn't realize how distant I was becoming and failed to recognize that my kids would act out for attention because I wasn't spending quality time with them. I didn't realize that every time I would carry my baby boy around the house, I would look for every opportunity to pass him off to someone else so I could go somewhere, just to be alone. And I especially failed to realize how rejected my wife would feel because of my inability to look her in the eyes. I was bitter in my life and blind to the fact I was hurting the ones I loved. At least, I was, until this February evening, when I stepped out onto the deck to barbeque dinner.

I remember this particular evening as if it were yesterday: It was cold outside, but tolerable in the absence of the wind. I was out in a spring jacket, but warmed by the heat of the barbeque. I turned to admire the snow covered landscape in the backyard. I clearly remember the serenity in the atmosphere that night as snowflakes gently descended from the clouds above. It looked nice, but it did little to alleviate the pain I was feeling in my heart.

A knocking sound startled me and I snapped back to my conscious world. My six-year-old daughter was banging her hands on the patio door, gesturing that she wanted to come outside with me. I smiled at her and nodded. She turned away and ran off toward the closet to put her snowsuit on. I redirected my attention toward the barbeque and took a number of deep breaths to calm the anxiety and heaviness I was feeling. I heard the door slam from the side of the house and in my peripheral, watched my daughter run toward the deck. As I reflect back on that night, I remember hearing my daughter's voice when she spoke to me, but I have no recollection of what she said. I just remember fading in and out of conscious thought. Although she was only a few feet away from me, I felt distant from her in my thoughts. Then it was quiet. I turned to see if she was still there, and she was, lounging in a pile of snow behind me. She looked up and smiled. I returned the smile and refocused on my culinary duty.

Then she asked me something that would forever change my life:
"Daddy?" she said.
"Yeah," I responded.
In her soft voice, she asked:
"When you get better, can you build a snowman with me?"

I will never forget how it felt when those words registered with my consciousness. It felt like a mushroom cloud of emotion erupted inside me. And in this moment, it felt as though my heart broke in two. I raised my head and gazed into the distance as tears swelled in my eyes. Before I could answer her, I had to clear the lump in my throat as it took all I had to keep it together, emotionally. I remember feeling the warmth of my tears streaming down the side of my cold cheeks as I answered her.

"I-I would like that," I said softly. "I would like that very much."

I turned my head slightly and watched as she skipped off the deck and disappeared around the corner of the house. I sobbed briefly and then pulled myself together before heading in with dinner. Her words echoed inside my head as I ate, and I don't remember if I said a single word at the table. When I finished, I told my wife that I was going to the basement to play guitar for a bit before helping to clean up. I went down the steps and made my way to the dim lit corner of our basement where my guitar was standing. I sat down and gripped an E-minor chord, but I couldn't play. All I could think about was what my daughter had said to me outside on the deck. I tried to push her words away from my thoughts, but I couldn't. After a few minutes, I heard footsteps coming down the stairs. My wife turned the corner and smiled at me as I sat there, holding my guitar.

She asked me if I was feeling okay and I responded untruthfully, that I was. I gripped the E-minor chord again, and as I began to pick away on my guitar, I broke down. I couldn't suppress my emotions any longer. My wife came over and put her arms around me and held me tight. I buried my face into her shoulder and bawled, flushing out the emotional turmoil that had overwhelmed me for so long. I couldn't stop shaking as I admitted to her that I was struggling in my life. I told her that I had convinced myself that she and the kids would be better off without me, and that I had nothing more to give them. She held me tight, affirming her love and our children's love for me, urging that I find the courage to seek help. I pulled myself together and lifted my face off of her shoulder and wiped away my tears.

I looked at her and told her what my daughter had said to me on the deck, and broke down again.

"She's six years old." I cried.

"The kids know," my wife assured, "They may not understand what it is that's hurting you, but they know there's something wrong with their father. There is nothing to be ashamed of."

"I'm scared." I cried. "I just want it to stop. I just want it all to stop."

After a few moments and a few deep breaths, I wiped the tears from my eyes and told my wife I would call my doctor.

11

Trapped inside a deep, dark well

It was in this moment that I realized I was sick and I truly needed help. I was suffering from a condition called *major depressive disorder* or what is commonly referred to as *depression*. It is difficult to explain in words what it is like to live with depression, but the best way I can describe my experience is in the figurative context of being trapped inside a deep well.

It feels like you are immersed in darkness, treading the still, black water in the depths. In this place, you feel alone and detached from the outside world, uninterested in its events. Ill-conceived notions about your life's circumstances pull you under as you struggle to stay afloat. The problems and challenges you face in your life are magnified by distorted perception, so large that they appear insufferable. You feel overwhelmed within the tight confines of the walls that incapacitate you, and it becomes a struggle to carry out the most basic functions of daily living, like eating, sleeping and at times, breathing. Unresolved symptoms of this mental disorder intensify and contaminate how you think and what you believe about yourself and the world around you.

You feel hopeless, and with clouded perception, you question your own significance in life. In this contaminated mindset, your cognitive ability to distinguish between rational and irrational thinking fades, leading to impaired judgement when contemplating ways to make the suffering stop. And it is in this state, void of one's cognitive defenses, where the unthinkable becomes thinkable.

Symptoms are manageable

Today, when I reflect back on that time when I had viewed my life with genuine indifference, it disturbs me greatly. This is because the landscape now looks so much different than it did the night my little girl reached out to me. Today, I do not feel trapped in the figurative deep, dark well of depression. Rather, I feel like I am standing on top of the well, exposed to the Sun's radiating warmth, liberated from *depressive oppression.*

The problems and challenges in my life that I once perceived were *insufferable*, I now recognize are *manageable.* The unrelenting emotions of guilt and regret that consumed me for everything that I believed went wrong in my life, I now hold in disregard. The most disheartening belief that *my family would be better without me* – one I had embraced in a very unstable mindset – I now view in disdain. And the feeling of hopelessness that served to weaken my cognitive defenses, I have negated with purpose. Today, I feel healthy.

Healing is a journey

My journey toward achieving liberation from the symptoms of major depressive disorder began at a critical point in my depressive episode and nearly two years later, I was able to break free from the shackles of mental oppression. This book describes the pathway I followed in the time it took me to get mentally healthy. And it serves as a testament to my said purpose, which is to share with others who may be struggling in this disorder, a self-proven approach to healing in depression and overcoming its debilitating symptoms.

13

An approach

I do want to make clear that this pathway I speak of is *an* approach to healing and is not to be interpreted as *the* approach. Personally, I do not believe such an approach exists. In my experience having lived with this disorder, and based on many months of research and counselling, I have learned that there is no magical cure. And unlike enduring a physical fracture, major depression is not so easily diagnosed. Therefore, the most effective treatment methods can be difficult to determine due to the intangible nature of this disorder.

What I do know, however, is that my journey toward overcoming depressive symptoms required me to leverage two very important fundamentals: *being proactive* and *being responsible*. My approach is *proactive* because it requires that you accept the condition that you must do the work in order to put your journey into motion; and it is *responsible* because it requires you to accept full ownership of the very choices, and resulting consequences, that you not only make, but have made in your life.

Healing is difficult

I can speak from experience that the journey toward achieving liberation from depressive symptoms is not easy. There are no short cuts and there will be significant challenges along the way. But my promise to you is that if you are prepared to pay the price for your freedom from this mental disorder, from its debilitating symptoms, then I assure you there is hope and there is a way out. I offer you my approach to healing and overcoming symptoms of depression, and this book will serve to guide you each and every step of the way.

I understand that I do not know your circumstances. But I can relate intimately to the painful and relentless emotions that radiate from this disorder. I can relate to that pain you feel in your heart when you believe you are alone in this world, that you have no one to turn to, or are convinced that the people you love would be better off without you. I can relate to the emptiness you feel because you believe you have let everyone down. I can relate to the tears you shed when you are alone with your thoughts, overwhelmed by the perceived pressures of life's challenges. I can relate to enduring emotions of sorrow, regret, and guilt that torment you for every perceived wrong decision you blame yourself for in your life. And if you think that you are in such a hopeless place right now, convinced that you cannot be saved, then believe me when I tell you that I can especially relate to that deep, dark place in depression where you contemplate unthinkable ways to make the hurting stop.

There is hope, always

I feel that I can relate to you in this disorder on many levels. Although I may not know your personal circumstances, your trials and tribulations, I do know that no matter how hopeless you perceive things to be in your life, there is *hope*. There is always hope. I am offering you hope in this book, in the form of an approach that has helped me overcome the debilitating symptoms of major depressive disorder.

I believe that the secret to your success in overcoming oppression in this disorder lies in an unconditional freedom that you and I, and every other person on this planet, innately possess: *the freedom to choose.* You own the power to make choices in your life, in any circumstance, and you have the freedom to leverage this power *proactively* and *responsibly.* But it is up to you to make that choice, to choose to commence your journey to overcoming symptoms of depression.

Your journey begins by simply *choosing* to turn the page.

PREFACE

G.E.T. HEALTHY: THE BEGINNING

BACKGROUND

Before I begin to outline my approach to healing in depression, I believe it is necessary to first establish some context with respect to how this approach came to fruition. Shortly after my daughter reached out to me that night, I made the first proactive and responsible choice that set my journey into motion: I called my doctor. Following a difficult assessment, my doctor referred me for psychiatric counselling, and I spent the next thirteen months of my life in professional care. I saw my therapist about every two to three weeks during this period, although weekly sessions were not uncommon, determined by the severity of my condition at the time.

In addition to scheduled sessions with my therapist, I expressed myself in writing, at first for therapeutic purposes. I wrote about what was going through my mind and about the feelings I was experiencing, towards myself, my family and life in general. I wrote about difficult life experiences that I believed were to blame for my sickness.

I grew hungry for knowledge and sought to learn as much as I could about my disorder. I visited mental health association websites and a multitude of other online sources. I researched academic reports on the topic of depression and anything else that would help me better understand what I was truly dealing with.

Over time, I began to form new perceptions and beliefs about this disorder and about life in general, and wrote about them. I created conceptual ideas as to what this disorder would look like if I could *see* it or *touch* it; and created a measurable perspective that I was able to relate to my own depression.

Throughout my writing and research efforts, I discovered ways in which I could be proactive and things that I could do for myself to help counter my depressive symptoms. I uncovered life changing principles that transformed how I thought and what I believed, about myself, my challenges, and the world around me.

My belief system became transformed, from one that was reactive and self-limiting, to a system that was *proactive* and *responsible*. I established a goal, something that I could look forward to, and this served as a tremendous source of empowerment throughout my journey in healing. In time, the very symptoms that had such a tight grip on my life began to loosen. And for the first time in my struggle with this disorder, I was able to see the light. I had discovered hope.

I shared and discussed much of what I wrote with my therapist during the time I was in counselling. At times, he would challenge my thought processes – my beliefs and interpretations – and helped strengthen my rational and logical capacities. I filtered his feedback into my writing, making adjustments where needed until it all started to come together.

Where I was once disoriented in this disorder, like trying to make sense of ten thousand puzzle pieces scattered about, things started to fall into place. The puzzle began to take shape. I was beginning to understand this disorder; not only why it was affecting me, but what I could do to effectively counter its debilitating symptoms. Where I was once hopeless and trapped in that deep well, I was able to see a way out. And in my healing, I discovered purpose: *to help those who are suffering like I was, see what I was able to see so they could do what I was eventually going to do: overcome symptoms of depression.*

I realized that I could fulfill my said purpose by presenting my approach to healing in the form of a book. This would provide me with a tool to leverage to fulfill my purpose. And this is how my approach, the idea behind this book came to fruition. So what began as a therapeutic exercise in writing grew into a catalyst of hope and liberation from symptoms of depression.

OVERALL THEME: G.E.T. HEALTHY!

In thinking about an overall theme for my book, the acronym *G.E.T.* came to mind. It represents what I would categorize are three progressive stages to healing in depression, based on my own personal experience:

"G" stands for: Gain Knowledge;

"E" stands for: Establish Perspective; and

"T" stands for: Take Action.

The overall theme of my book was born. My approach to healing in depression: simply, *G.E.T. Healthy!*

The First Stage: Gain Knowledge

The first stage of my approach to effectively manage and overcome depressive symptoms requires that we leverage the power of *knowledge*. It is my belief that the more we learn about depression and its debilitating symptoms, the more effective we can be in managing them.

"Know thy self, know thy enemy. A thousand battles, a thousand victories." - Sun Tzu, *The Art of War*

In this stage, we will define what depression is and what it is not. We will discuss what I refer to as the *grey area* of depression, based on the belief that *sickness in mind* is far more difficult to recognize, diagnose, and treat than *sickness in body*. We will identify the many causes of depression, its symptoms and severities. And finally, I will introduce my *Depression Severity Range Scale Model* – a tool I used to gain a conceptual measure of severity associated with my own depression.

Gaining knowledge about this disorder prepares us for the second stage of the *G.E.T. Healthy!* approach to overcoming symptoms of depression:

21

The Second Stage: Establish Perspective

Establishing *perspective* requires that we leverage the knowledge we gained in the first stage to help establish a proactive and responsible process of thinking. The goal of this stage is to establish and adopt three fundamental beliefs about this disorder and our own personal circumstances:

Perspective #1: Depression is a place that has a way out.

The purpose of this perspective is to not only establish a conceptual understanding of what it is like living with depression, but to establish a *condition of hope* in this disorder. I believe that adopting this first perspective is critical to effectively managing symptoms because unless we are somehow able to replace this 'dark place' in depression with a perspective with defined and relatable features, it remains a dark, mysterious place with no conceivable way out. The danger in this type of thinking is that it cultivates *hopelessness*, a debilitating symptom of depression.

In my approach, I describe depression in the figurative context of being trapped in a deep, dark well. This metaphor best illustrates my perception of what it is like living with this disorder. In Chapter 3, I will identify and discuss the conceptual features that make up the anatomy of this dark well, particularly the *ladder*, which I believe serves as a symbol of *hope* in our journey.

"If we climb high enough, we will reach a height from which tragedy ceases to look tragic." — Irvin D. Yalom, *When Nietzsche Wept*

Perspective #2: Your circumstances are not the worst case.

The purpose of this perspective is to establish what one might consider by today's standards, a *worst-case* scenario in depression, or in other words, an extreme standard for suffering against which we can measure our own depressive experience. The extent of our physical, emotional and spiritual suffering associated with depression is relative and individual, and in the absence of something comparable to relate our suffering to, we may perceive our problems to be larger than perhaps what they truly are. And in a contaminated state of mind, we may even perceive them to be larger than life itself.

The extreme standard for suffering that I leveraged for my own purpose, and one I am introducing in the *G.E.T. Healthy!* approach, is based on Austrian psychiatrist and Holocaust survivor Viktor E. Frankl's account of prisoner life in Nazi concentration camps. Although our incarceration with respect to depression is figurative in context, Frankl's confinement was very real.

I embraced this perspective because I was able to recognize many parallels from Frankl's accounts between prisoner life in concentration camps and the *incarceration* one feels when oppressed by depressive symptoms. I was able to extract and leverage important principles from Frankl's personal experience to help me better manage my own struggles with depression. One such principle serves as the basis for the third perspective of my *G.E.T. Healthy!* approach:

23

Perspective #3: You possess the freedom to choose.

The purpose of this perspective is to leverage what Frankl describes as "the last of the human freedoms," the very principle owing to his survival and eventual liberation from Nazi confinement. According to Frankl, it was the one and only thing that he and every other prisoner possessed that not even his captives could take away from them: the freedom "…to choose one's attitude in any given set of circumstances, to choose one's own way."[1]

Frankl was able to overcome extreme mental, physical and spiritual anguish throughout his ordeal because he chose to leverage this freedom. In the most horrific of circumstances, he chose his own way.

You will learn in Chapter 6 that you possess this very same freedom. Furthermore, you will learn how to leverage this power to help you overcome *oppression in depression*. You will learn how to leverage a proactive and responsible attitude in what you might perceive is the worst of circumstances in your life. In the context of the *G.E.T. Healthy!* approach, you will learn that the *freedom to choose* is the single most important principle that you will leverage before progressing onto the final stage of your journey to healing in depression:

The Third Stage: Take Action

The third and final stage to healing in depression is taking *action*. Gaining knowledge in Stage 1 and establishing proactive and responsible perspectives in Stage 2 prepares us mentally for the third and final stage of the *G.E.T. Healthy!* approach. Based on my own personal experience,

I identify seven action steps to achieving liberation from depressive symptoms:

Step 1: 'Defibrillate' your depression

Imagine a person going into cardiac arrest. The paramedics apply a defibrillator which sends a thousand volts of electric shock through the victim's body in hopes of reviving his still heart long enough for doctors to stabilize him. This is similar to what we aim to accomplish in the first action step toward healing in depression.

The underlying principle in this first step is that *your feelings and emotions are determined by your thoughts and beliefs*. When you have a *negative* belief or perception about a specific situation in your life, this, in turn, produces *negative* emotions which can cultivate certain depressive symptoms. The *G.E.T. Healthy!* approach shows you how to trigger an emotional eruption within your heart.

In Chapter 9, I will show you how to leverage your defibrillator moment in depression. When you experience this, it will open up that critical small window of opportunity in your mental oppression to escape and advance to the second, *stabilizing* step of the *G.E.T. Healthy!* approach:

Step 2: Get help

The second step toward healing in depression is to get help, or specifically, call your doctor. While this may appear to be an obvious step to those who have never struggled with depression, it was, in my own personal experience, an extremely difficult step to take.

Depression is a condition that carries with it a perceived stigma, and this alone can be enough to deter a person from seeking professional help. My *defibrillator* moment in depression subconsciously lowered my defenses and in that moment, I could see with clarity that I was sick and that my loved ones were hurting for me. It exposed me to a crossroads at which I had to make a choice: either be *reactive* and choose to do nothing, surrendering to the debilitating symptoms of this disorder, or be *proactive*, take *responsibility* and choose to make the call to seek professional help.

In Chapter 10, I will share the framework that helped me transition from a reactive mindset to one that is proactive and responsible. And it is this new process of thinking that will provide the necessary momentum to take that third step toward healing in depression:

Step 3: Forgive yourself

The feeling of *guilt* is identified by health professionals as a symptom of depression and this served as one of the most debilitating symptoms I had to contend with. The third step toward healing in this disorder requires that we learn to genuinely forgive ourselves for any regretful choices we have made in the past.

In Chapter 11, I will introduce the Ghost of Guilt paradigm and teach you how to leverage a proactive approach to not only forgiving yourself, but forgiving others for any wrong-doings that we may blame for our conditions. This may be perceived as the most difficult hurdle to overcoming symptoms on this journey, but I believe it is essential in our healing that we genuinely find peace in our hearts before we can fully leverage the next step of the *G.E.T. Healthy!* approach:

Step 4: Create a goal to look forward to

The fourth step requires us to make a proactive and dynamic shift in mental focus, from living in the past to living for the future. The fundamental purpose of this step is to instill meaning and purpose in your life, and in Chapter 12, we aim to accomplish this by creating a goal to look forward to. I believe this is a critical step in the healing process because as long as you have a goal to strive for, you will have something in your life to look forward to, despite your circumstances. This creates proactive momentum that will not only help you to effectively manage depressive symptoms, but will provide considerable leverage in the preservation of your mental health.

We will also acknowledge an irrefutable truth in life: *you cannot change the past.* Or in other words:

"The Moving Finger writes; and, having writ, moves on: nor all thy piety nor Wit shall lure it back to cancel half a Line, Nor all thy Tears wash out a Word of it." - Omar Khayyam

Furthermore, we will recognize that there are valuable life lessons we can take from past experiences, regardless of how they are perceived – and when leveraged proactively and responsibly – can serve to improve our lives today and in the future. This leads us to the next step of the *G.E.T. Healthy!* approach:

Step 5: Leverage exercise to alleviate depressive symptoms

Our focus up until now has been on making proactive and responsible adjustments to our *minds*, specifically in how we think – our beliefs and perspectives. In this step, we aim to counter symptoms of depression by leveraging the direct physiological and psychological benefits produced by physical exercise.

I have discovered in my research that there exists a mountain of empirical evidence supporting the effectiveness of exercise training in treating depressive symptoms – and it continues to grow. We will learn in Chapter 13 that in some studies, physical exercise is considered just as, if not more effective, than antidepressant medication.

We will also discuss how symptoms of depression affect the body's physiology, particularly the chemical processes that take place which influences how we feel in this disorder. In addition, we will identify the inherent, longer-term health risks associated with unresolved symptoms. The next step of the *G.E.T. Healthy!* approach:

Step 6: Embrace the good in your life

We are now stronger in our physical and mental capacities after having progressed through the first five steps of the *G.E.T. Healthy!* approach. Step Six is the point where, in our deep well context, we pull ourselves up and out of the well of depression. At this point in our healing, we focus on life's blessings – specifically, the things that bring meaning and value to our lives.

The underlying purpose of this chapter is to leverage everything you have learned in the preceding steps to establish a foundation of productive beliefs. This proactive and responsible process of thinking can position us to deal more effectively with challenges that we currently face and condition us to better cope with challenges we have yet to encounter. In this proactive mindset, we are prepared to take the final step toward healing in depression:

Step 7: Give back and help others

It was at this point – the very last step of a long journey to healing – that I discovered what I would consider is the single most powerful action to liberating oneself from the oppressive forces of depression: *giving back*. In other words, you must commit to be a difference maker in the lives of others, or someone, or something else. By committing to be a difference maker in this world, not just casually, but consistently, we cultivate *purpose* and *meaning* in our lives. In Chapter 15, I will share with you my framework to help you find your place as a difference maker in this disorder.

STAGE 1

GAIN KNOWLEDGE

CHAPTER 1

Defining Depression

Prior to learning intimately about what depression truly is, I used to consider *depression* as a seemingly natural emotion that we feel when we're down in the dumps, so to speak. If I mess up at work, I may feel discouraged and *depressed;* or if I act impatiently with the kids, I may feel guilty and *depressed;* or if I can't afford to take the family on an expensive vacation, I may feel inadequate and *depressed;* and so on. Back then, I would use the term *depression* interchangeably with negative emotions such as sadness or grief. I have learned that *depression* is not *natural* or *normal.* Nor is it an emotion. So what really is this thing called *depression?*

31

When I first began my research in 2012, the Canadian Mental Health Association (CMHA) described depression as: "A major depressive disorder-usually just called "depression"-is different than the "blues". Someone experiencing depression is grappling with feelings of severe despair over an extended period of time. Almost every aspect of their life can be affected, including their emotions, physical health, relationships and work. For people with depression, it does not feel like there is a 'light at the end of the tunnel'-there is just a long, dark tunnel."[2]

CMHA has since revised their description which, as of June 2018, reads: "…a type of mental illness called a mood disorder. Mood disorders affect the way you feel, which also affects the way you think and act. With depression, you may feel 'down,' hopeless, or find that you can't enjoy things you used to like. Many people who experience depression feel irritable or angry. And some people say that they feel 'numb' all the time."

Mental Health America defines Major Depressive Disorder (Clinical Depression) as: "a mental health condition characterized by an inescapable and ongoing low mood often accompanied by low self-esteem and loss of interest or pleasure in activities that a person used to find enjoyable. To meet the criteria for Major Depressive Disorder (MDD), symptoms must be present nearly every day for at least 2 weeks. MDD is also often referred to as Major Depression."[3]

Merriam-Webster Dictionary defines depression as: "A psychoneurotic or psychotic disorder marked especially by sadness, inactivity, difficulty in thinking and concentration, a significant increase or decrease in appetite and time spent sleeping, feelings of dejection and hopelessness, and sometimes suicidal tendencies."

DEPRESSION IS A DISORDER

Do you see what each of these definitions has in common? They each identify depression as a disorder. Let's look at the key words and phrases in each definition that would not apply to what otherwise could be described as a natural human emotion. Firstly, depression is a mental *disorder* whereas *sadness* is an emotion, or alternatively, a mental *reaction* to an unfavorable circumstance.

Secondly, depression is marked by *inactivity* or a deficit in one's ability to function normally on a daily basis. Feeling sad does not inhibit your ability to get out of bed in the morning, although you may *feel* like you don't want to get up because you feel 'blah'. But you can get up and carry on with your daily routine despite feeling sad, and when a positive experience does occur in your day, the emotion of sadness is generally displaced by favorable emotions, like happiness and joy. But with depression, the actual physical act of getting up and out of a bed can be inhibited by certain debilitating symptoms.

Thirdly, and perhaps the most distinctive factor, is the reference to *time*. In CMHA's earlier definition, it reads: "Someone experiencing depression is grappling with feelings of severe despair over an extended period of time." We all experience a variety of natural human emotions throughout the course of a day, like happiness, excitement, frustration, anger, and disappointment, to name a few. But for someone struggling with depression, undesirable emotions can linger on for prolonged periods of time.

DEPRESSION IS COMPLEX

I have learned from experience and research that depression is a very complex and complicated disorder. When I came to the realization that I was struggling with a mental illness, I didn't at that time appreciate the severity of my condition. This is because it was not easily measurable.

Through research and discussions with my therapist, I learned to appreciate that diagnosing, treating and healing *sickness of mind* is considerably more difficult than diagnosing, treating and healing *sickness of body*. There is no x-ray technology that can pinpoint the precise reason as to why and how a person *feels* the way they do.

When one is diagnosed with cancer, the first logical question that would come to mind is, *how far along is it?* Or, *how bad is it?* Medical tests will not only determine the stage the cancer is in, but will point medical professionals to the best treatment options available for the patient. Furthermore, there is no particular treatment or drug that can heal a *broken mental state* in the same manner that a cast can heal a broken arm, or a chemotherapeutic drug can eliminate cancer cells. In both of these *physical* references, the patient is fully aware of her symptoms, and remains fully dependent on direct medical responses in the form of a cast or prescription medication to treat the physical ailment.

The science of human anatomy is generally consistent from person to person, however, belief systems and thought processes can differ greatly from one person to the next. This results in significant challenges for mental health professionals when diagnosing depression and determining its severity. As a consequence, there is no clear test to determine what the most effective method of treatment is for patients suffering with this mental disorder.

DEPRESSION IS CAUSED BY MANY THINGS

Another factor owing to the complexity of diagnosing and treating depression is the broad range of possible causes that can trigger this disorder. According to Mental Health America, there are many things that can contribute to depression:

Possible Causes of Depression

Biological	Chemical imbalance of certain brain chemicals
Cognitive	Negative thinking patterns and low self-esteem
Gender	Due to hormonal changes (i.e. menstruation, pregnancy, childbirth and menopause) and stress.
Co-occurrence	Depression can occur along with certain illnesses such as heart disease, cancer, Parkinson's disease, etc.
Medications	Side effects of some medications can bring about depression
Genetic	A family history of clinical depression increases the risk for developing the illness.
Situational	Difficult life events, including divorce, financial problems or the death of a loved one can contribute to depression.
No apparent reason	?

Source: Mental Health America. Retrieved from: http://www.mentalhealthamerica.net

There exist many possible causes of depression. The deterioration of one's mental state could be the result of a single cause or a combination of those identified above. In the words of my therapist, finding the root cause or causes of depression can be "like trying to find a needle in a haystack."

DEPRESSION IS MEASURABLE

I have learned in my research that there exists a checklist of symptoms that health professionals use when diagnosing depression and determining its severity in patients. These will be identified and discussed in more detail in Chapter 2. I have also learned of the different treatment options available for those struggling with depressive symptoms, which include but are not limited to psychotherapy (i.e. analyzing feelings and emotions, and internal belief systems); and anti-depressant medication.

MIXED FEELINGS ABOUT MEDICATION

Unlike the functionality of a cast, which supports in the healing process of a broken bone, the use of antidepressant medication, in my opinion, does not serve as a *healing* function, but rather a *treating* function. Based on my own personal experience, I believe that the actual healing process in this disorder is ultimately the patient's responsibility. I would like to qualify, however, that I certainly believe there are instances when prescribing antidepressant medication may be an appropriate response. The point is, with or without prescription medication, I believe that it is the patient who must be proactive in their disorder and leverage the support systems that exist when dealing with symptoms of depression.

PREPARE FOR BATTLE

I believe that the more we learn about the debilitating symptoms of depression, the more effective we can be in managing and overcoming them. Depression is a mental illness that can affect every area of your life. I have learned that depression is a very complex disorder, one that commands a great deal of respect for its inherent and debilitating dangers. Depression, we have learned, can be caused by many things, and can occur without reason.

My hope as you are reading this is that you too have gained a better understanding of this disorder. I sincerely hope that this information provides you with some sense of awareness in what it is that you may be dealing with or, perhaps, what somebody you care for may be struggling with. I believe that the more we learn about this inherent enemy called *depression,* and the more aware we become of its dangers, the more effective we can be in overcoming its debilitating symptoms.

"Know thy self, know thy enemy. A thousand battles, a thousand victories." - Sun Tzu, *The Art of War*

CHAPTER 2

Symptoms and Severity of Depression

The purpose of this chapter is twofold: first, to distinguish the varying *severities* of depression; and second, to identify the specific *symptoms* of depression. The information presented in this chapter is derived from academic research and journals on the subject of depression severity and associated symptoms. Through my research, I have identified three main categories of depression severity, and eight primary symptoms that are used by medical professionals when determining depression severity in patients.

THREE CATEGORIES OF DEPRESSION

Three categories of depression, listed from lowest severity to highest: *dysthymic* disorder, *minor depressive* disorder and *major depressive* disorder. I present these in the following visual, which I call the Depression Severity Range Scale:

Depression Severity Range Scale

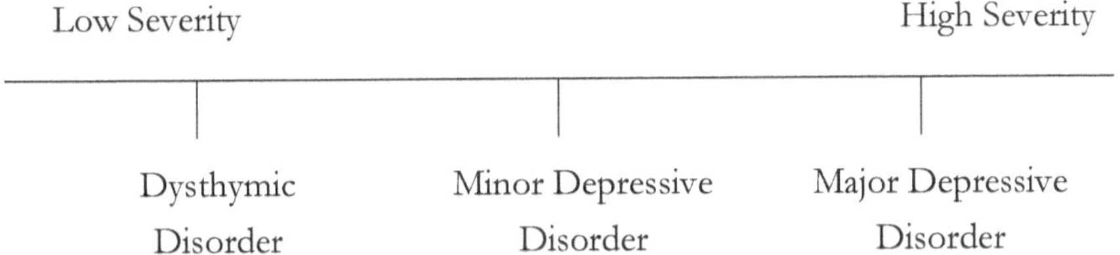

EIGHT SYMPTOMS OF DEPRESSION

Eight primary symptoms of depression used by health care professionals in diagnosing depression and determining its severity:

1. Sleep disorder (either increased or decreased sleep)*
2. Interest deficit (anhedonia)
3. Guilt (worthlessness*, hopelessness*, regret)
4. Energy deficit*
5. Concentration deficit*
6. Appetite disorder (either decreased or increased)*
7. Psychomotor retardation or agitation
8. Suicidality

"ARE YOU DEPRESSED?"

In one academic article[4], the author indicates that by simply asking an individual "Are you depressed?" was an effective screening method for depression. If the individual responded with *"Yes"*, then the next step was to determine the presence of symptoms, or in medical terms, the presence of *neurovegetative symptoms*. The author distinguishes between low severity in depression and high severity in depression based on the following conditions:

Low severity in depression: "To meet the diagnosis of <u>dysthymic disorder</u>, a patient must have two of the six symptoms marked with an asterisk, plus depression, for at least two years."[5]

High severity in depression: "To meet the diagnosis of <u>major depression</u>, a patient must have four of the symptoms plus depressed mood or anhedonia, for at least two weeks."[6]

With these defined conditions, the Depression Severity Range Scale introduced above can be expanded as follows:

Depression Severity Range Scale

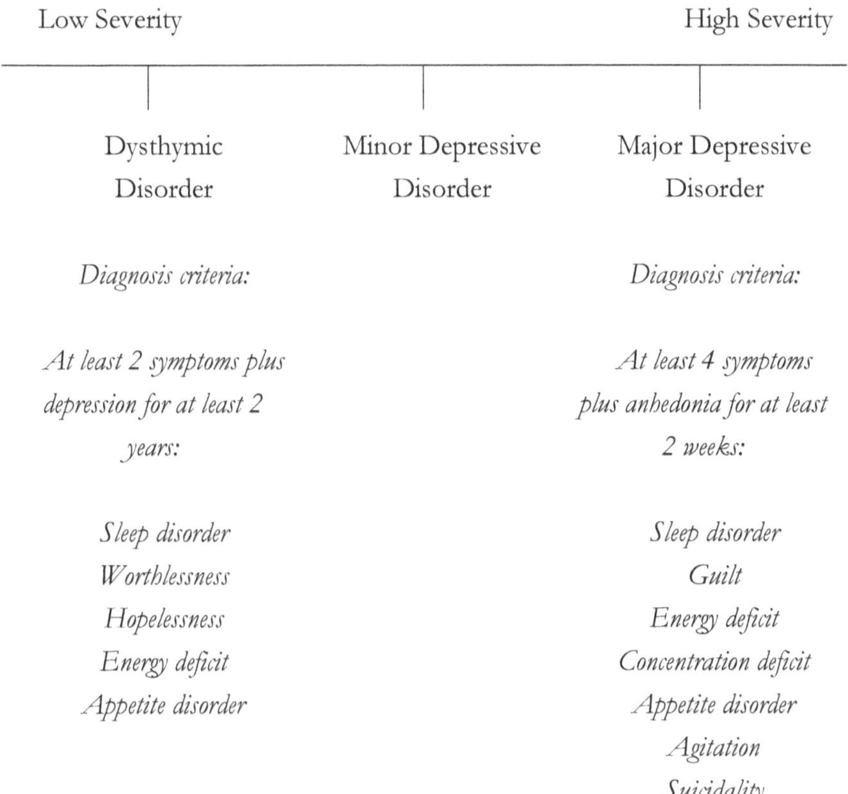

A third category called minor depression is defined in another article as: "…depressive conditions that are not of sufficient severity and duration to meet criteria for a major depressive episode."[7] The authors of the same article explain that minor depression is characterized more by *cognitive* symptoms and less by *neurovegetative* symptoms. A list of these cognitive symptoms is provided in the expanded model below:

Depression Severity Range Scale

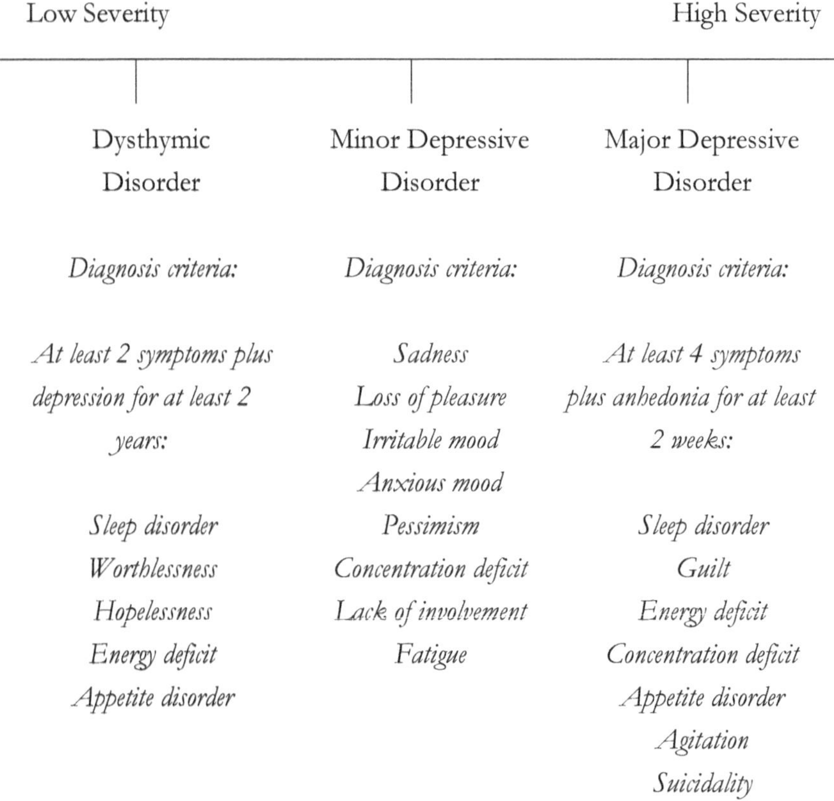

The authors distinguish *minor depression* from *major depression* by the *infrequent* occurrence of neurovegetative symptoms. A comparison of diagnosis criteria provided in the Depression Severity Range Scale shows three symptoms that are common in both *minor* and *major* depression: concentration deficit, interest deficit (or lack of involvement), and energy deficit (or fatigue). The authors acknowledge other studies that endorse neurovegetative symptoms over cognitive symptoms in the diagnosis of minor depression, with the inclusion of sleep disorder, appetite disorder, worthlessness and suicidality.

MINOR DEPRESSIVE DISORDER

Unlike dysthymia or major depressive disorder, the underlying criteria for diagnosing *minor depressive disorder* does not seem to be clearly defined. In fact, it could be argued that both the *cognitive* and *neurovegetative symptoms* listed under minor depression in some ways overlap with the more clearly defined symptoms of both *dysthymic disorder* and *major depressive disorder*. For example, *minor depression* appears to have one neurovegetative symptom in common with *dysthymic disorder* (i.e. energy deficit/fatigue) and three that are common to *major depression* (concentration deficit, lack of involvement/interest deficit, and energy deficit/fatigue). The diagnosis criteria unique to *minor depression* are the remaining cognitive symptoms listed.

With reference to the Depression Severity Range Scale on the previous page, it stands to reason that the severity of *minor* depression could possibly range closer in relative terms to dysthymic disorder if symptoms are more *cognitive* in nature (i.e. of low severity) and closer to major depressive disorder if symptoms are more *neurovegetative* in nature (i.e. of high severity). A somewhat balanced combination of both *cognitive* and *neurovegetative* symptoms could be conceptually located at the mid-point of the Depression Severity Range Scale.

The purpose of this chapter is not to debate the relevance of cognitive symptoms in depression, but rather to gain a broadened understanding of depression severity. I can say from personal experience that when I was formally diagnosed with *major depressive disorder*, I did struggle with

43

cognitive symptoms in unison with neurovegetative symptoms. This leads me to question the relevance of *minor depression* as a stand-alone measure of depression severity – in this context.

FROM DYSTHYMIA TO MAJOR DEPRESSION

For both *dysthymic* and *major depressive disorder*, each has its own set of distinct criteria that sets them apart, even though both share certain neurovegetative symptoms. As such, both are seemingly easy to measure along the conceptual Depression Severity Range Scale.

That is, dysthymia has a relatively limited range given restrictions to its diagnosis criteria (i.e. excludes specific, and relatively more serious neurovegetative symptoms like suicidality and psychomotor retardation). One can reason, then, that its range on the Depression Severity Range Scale, as illustrated at the bottom of the following diagram, would not reach beyond the mid-point of the scale (but would, however, overlap the *minor depressive* category at the mid-point).

Depression Severity Range Scale

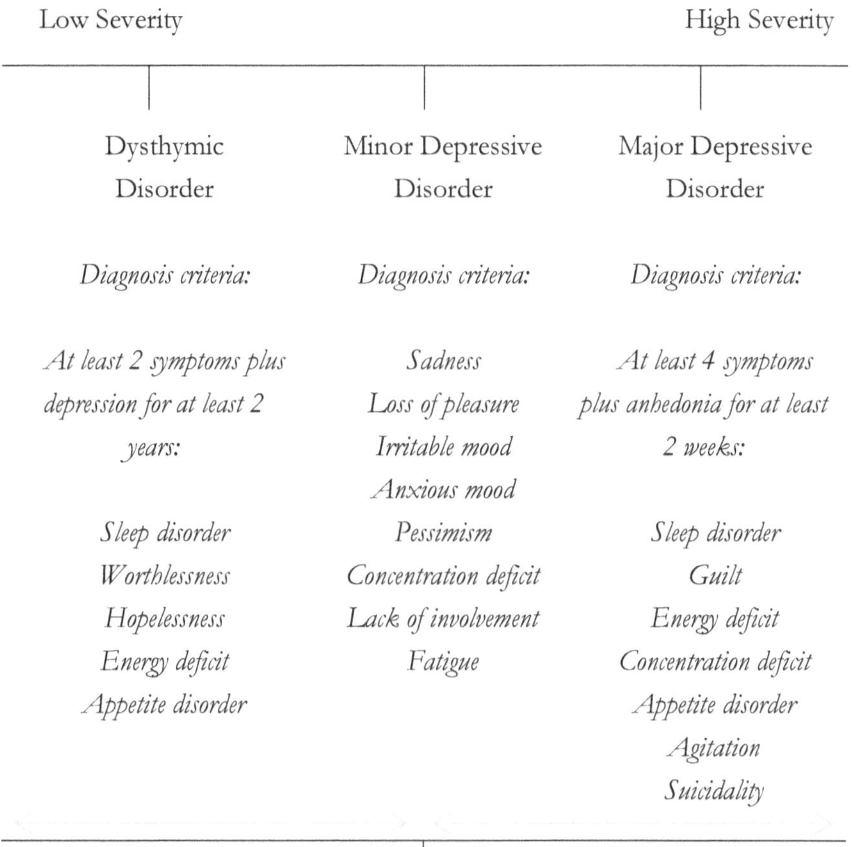

Likewise, given the less restrictive diagnosis criteria for *major depressive disorder* and the more serious neurovegetative symptoms that define it, its range can be thought to extend from the midpoint to the high severity portion of the scale. It stands to reason, then, that the Depression Severity Range Scale, which is a crude representation of relative severities between the three suggestive categories, can be condensed into the following model:

Depression Severity Range Scale

MEASURING DEPRESSION:
A PERSONAL PERSPECTIVE

Earlier in this chapter, I referenced an article in which the author indicated that simply asking, "Are you depressed?", was an effective screening method for depression. If the individual responded *"Yes"*, then the next step would be to determine the presence of *neurovegetative symptoms*.

In this exercise, I put myself in the shoes of that individual who is being asked the question: *Are you depressed?* My response, of course, is *Yes!* When I reflect back to that fateful evening when my daughter reached out to me, I knew that I was struggling with depression. I was, however, unaware of just how serious my condition was - at least until I went to see my family doctor. In that meeting, he asked some very difficult questions, and I responded with some very difficult answers. In hindsight, I now realize that his questions were formulated to determine the presence of *neurovegetative symptoms* in my depression. For simplicity purposes, the following represents my own personal checklist of depressive symptoms from my meeting with my doctor:

Personal Checklist of Neurovegetative Symptoms of Depression

(Note: symptoms denoted with an asterisk * are associated with determining dysthymic disorder)

✓ Sleep disorder (either increased or decreased sleep)*

✓ Interest deficit (anhedonia)

✓ Guilt (worthlessness*, hopelessness*, regret)

4. Energy deficit*

✓ Concentration deficit*

6. Appetite disorder (either decreased or increased)*

✓ Psychomotor retardation or agitation

✓ Suicidality

✓ Neurovegetative/depressed mood symptoms for a duration longer than two weeks

In determining the presence of neurovegetative symptoms associated with my depression, I would have checked six out of the eight symptoms listed. This more than meets the criteria required to diagnose major depressive disorder (requiring the presence of four

47

neurovegetative symptoms and depressed mood for more than two weeks).

In the context of the depression severity range model (below), my condition exceeded the diagnosis criteria for *dysthymic disorder*, thus indicating it was more severe – in the *major depression* range. This is illustrated by the dot arbitrarily placed on the *high severity* side of the scale:

Depression Severity Range Scale

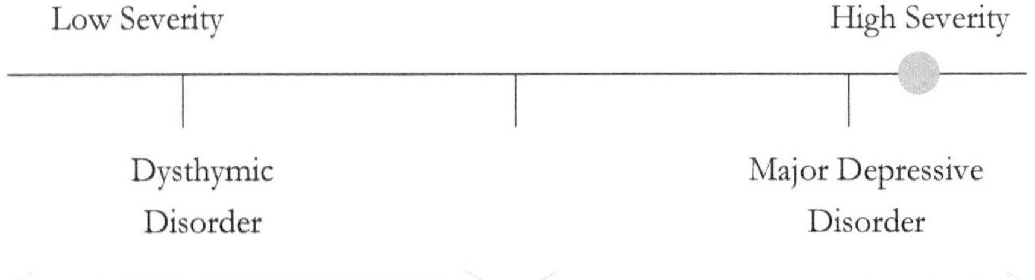

THE REALITY OF MEASURING DEPRESSION SEVERITY

This chapter provided a simple and conceptual representation of measuring severity in depression. The reality is that when you go through this process that a medical professional would use to determine the presence of neurovegetative symptoms, you can see that it's neither simple nor completely conceptual. It is very real. I can honestly say that this was the most difficult thing I ever had to go through in my life.

It was a terrifying experience. As difficult as the questions were, it was a struggle to communicate the answers back to my doctor. The trembling, the twitching, the stuttering, the multiple breakdowns…it is difficult to explain in words. I did realize at the conclusion of my appointment just how serious my depressive condition was when my doctor cautioned me that he would exercise his authority for intervention at any sign of threat, particularly toward myself. At the conclusion of our session, my doctor indicated that he would send my referral for psychiatric counseling as soon as possible.

When I left his office, I met my wife in the hallway and reached out for my three-month old son. I sat down on the bench, buried my face into his little shoulder, and bawled, flushing out whatever emotion I had left in my system.

This was my reality in measuring depression severity.

STAGE 2

ESTABLISH PERSPECTIVE

CHAPTER 3

A 'Deep Well' Perspective of Depression

In Chapter 1, I provided the Canadian Mental Health Association's former description of depression, reproduced here:

"A major depressive disorder-usually just called "depression"-is different than the "blues". Someone experiencing depression is grappling with feelings of severe despair over an extended period of time. Almost every aspect of their life can be affected, including their emotions, physical health, relationships and work. For people with

51

depression, it does not feel like there is a 'light at the end of the tunnel'- there is just a long, dark tunnel."

When I read this, I can understand how the CMHA would relate *depression* to a *"long, dark tunnel"*; however, when I reflect on my own personal experience in this disorder, I have difficulty relating to this metaphor. For example, my interpretation of a long, dark tunnel in relation to mental illness is that there are only two directions to go: to the left or to the right. So I envision myself sitting in the dark, feeling lost and disoriented, uncertain as to which direction I should go. The anatomy of this dark tunnel is undefined, and in the absence of any conceptual understanding about the many facets that comprise this disorder, it remains a mysterious, dark place. Personally, I perceive the *tunnel* metaphor as a catalyst for hopelessness.

THE DEEP WELL OF DEPRESSION

I spent a great deal of time throughout the course of my therapy reflecting on this disorder - this *dark place*, trying to conceptualize what it would look like if you could *see* it and *feel* it. The best depiction of depression, based on my own personal experience, was like being trapped inside a deep, dark well.

My approach to overcoming symptoms of depression leverages what I call *'Deep Well Perspective Healing'* – an approach requiring that we first gain a conceptual understanding of the components that make up the anatomy of this well. This exercise can prove to be beneficial in the healing process because it offers a visual of what depression would *look* like as if it were tangible, or something *observable*. In addition, we can perceive its internal features as a means to shed some *conceptual* light on

52

what is a dark and mysterious place. Perhaps the most important benefit of this exercise is the opportunity to create a catalyst for *hope* in a disorder characterized by *hopelessness*.

An artistic depiction of my Deep Well of Depression concept – and descriptions of its internal features – is presented below.

The Deep Well of Depression

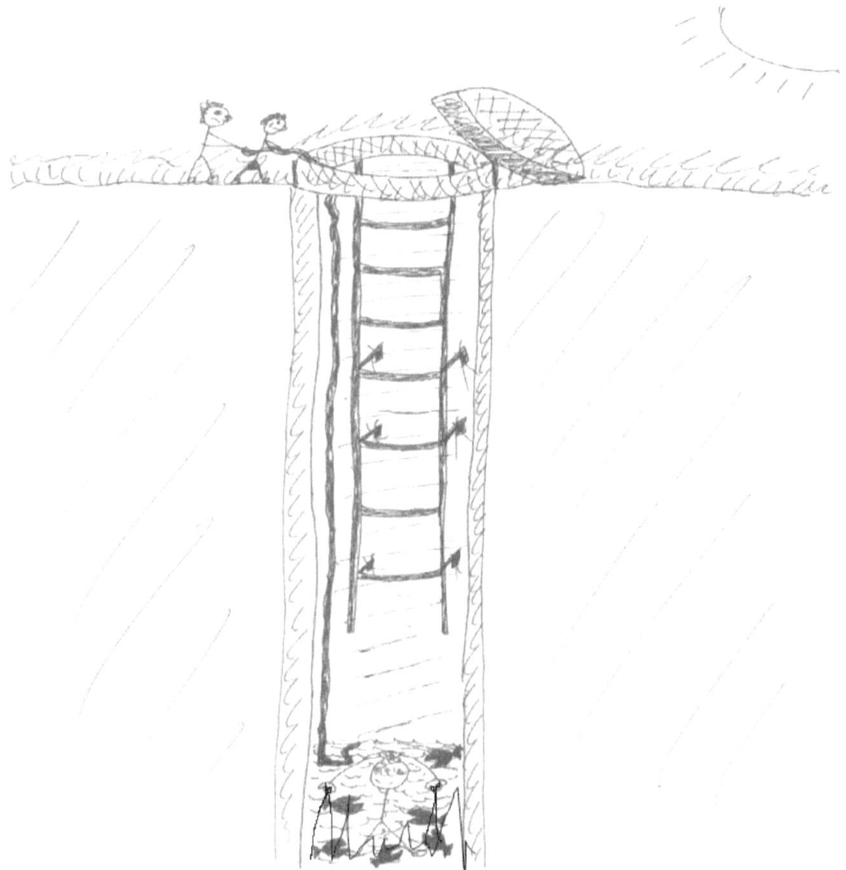

DEEP WELL OF DEPRESSION: CONCEPTUAL FEATURES

The Person (Treading Water)

The person treading water inside the deep, dark well represents what it's like living with depression. The person in the picture above is shown to have limited functionality, exerting just enough effort to stay afloat. His head is partially submerged under what I call the *Dark Water of Despair*, peering into the abyss below him. He lifts his head from time to time to fill his lungs with air before retreating back to his defeated state.

When he does lift his head, he fails to acknowledge the tiny beam of sunlight stretching down from the top of the well. At this depth, this beam is so tiny that it serves only as a frail reminder of any good in his life. With the exception of this tiny beam of light, he is engulfed in darkness.

In my personal experience, one depressive symptom from Chapter 2 that parallels the conceptual meaning behind the person treading the Dark Water of Despair is *interest deficit*. Simply, you lack interest in just about everything in your life. You are overcome by a sense of *defeatism* in response to life's challenges, which makes the simple task of getting out of bed in the morning difficult. You yearn to be alone. You shut the blinds, curl up in bed and cover yourself over with a blanket. From time to time, you observe sunlight beaming into your room through the cracks of the blinds, but fail to appreciate the seemingly beautiful day that exists on the other side of the window. Instead, you roll over and face the wall, cover your head, and cry.

Weeds of Damaging Beliefs

If you look closely at the person treading water inside the well, he is gripping in hand what looks to be weeds stemming from the bottom of the well. I call these Weeds of Damaging Beliefs, which symbolize a person's belief system in a state of depression. The weeds that the person in the picture is holding onto represent a contaminated belief system. He grips on to these weeds *tightly*, meaning he is determined in his beliefs, regardless of how hurtful they may be. As long as the person keeps holding on to these weeds, he will remain submerged in the depths of the well.

In my personal experience, I was holding onto many damaging beliefs about myself, and about how I was perceived by the world around me – especially by my family. I convinced myself that *my family was better off without me* and this cultivated the neurovegetative symptom of *hopelessness*. It wasn't until I was able to release my grip on those weeds that I could see clearly that that was not the case. Letting go of the Weeds of Damaging Beliefs is an essential condition to healing in this disorder.

Piranhas of Depression

In the diagram, notice next what appears to be fish surrounding the person treading the Dark Water of Despair. I refer to these fish as Piranhas of Depression, symbolizing the *sources* or *challenges* from which depressive symptoms originate.

In the Deep Well of Depression diagram, observe that the fish appear to be attracted to the presence of the person treading water. The fish surround him and strike while he struggles to stay afloat, vulnerable and

55

defenseless. Each successive strike by the Piranhas of Depression slowly wears him down, pushing him deeper into defeatism.

Upon closer examination of the picture, notice that there is a total of six piranhas in the Dark Water of Despair. Each piranha serves to represent a key area of life[8], specifically:

1. Family/home
2. Financial/career
3. Mental/educational
4. Physical/health
5. Social/cultural
6. Spiritual/ethical

The underlying concept is that all of life's challenges fall within the general boundaries of these six life areas. The benefit of identifying and presenting these life areas is that it gives us an opportunity to evaluate our problems or challenges by first observing the bigger picture. Conceptually, we can identify which life area generates the most pain, and then position ourselves to dig deeper into that life area in search of a root cause.

In the Deep Well of Depression, each life area is represented by a piranha circling the person in the water. For situational causes of depression, the *Family/home* piranha, for example, may be the one biting because of a divorce situation; or the *Financial/career* piranha could be most aggressive due to a recent job loss or financial problems. Similarly, for biological causes, the *Physical/health* piranha serves to represent chemical imbalances or hormonal factors that can contribute to depression.

One characteristic relating to the Piranhas of Depression is that in this figurative setting, not all six piranhas necessarily attack simultaneously. The aggressive behavior of these fish is dependent upon how *hungry* they are, or alternatively, determined by those that are *starved* the most.

For example, my depression may be triggered by a situational cause, like a divorce situation. However, in another area, such as *Financial/career*, I may be well off. Treading the Dark Water of Despair, I would be tormented by the *Family/home* piranha while the *Financial/career* piranha swims around, unmoved by my presence.

This may be because in reality, I spent all of my time focused on my career, making money (i.e. *feeding* the *Financial/career* piranha) while at the same time, neglecting the needs of my family (i.e. *starving* the *Family/home* piranha). Having neglected this area of my life for so long, the *Family/home* piranha is starved and reacts to my presence in the Dark Water of Despair with vicious intensity. As a result, my problems in this life area become magnified, perhaps larger than they should be perceived. The pain intensifies to such a degree that it becomes increasingly difficult to appreciate the good that exists in other life areas.

When you struggle with depression, your perceived problems and challenges can be all-encompassing. They become the first thing you think of when you wake in the morning and are what keeps you awake late at night. When left unresolved, the merciless attacks by the Piranhas of Depression can become incredibly overwhelming, so much so that symptoms can serve to weaken your cognitive defenses when contemplating ways to make the hurting stop.

The Sun

Earlier in this chapter, I made reference to the tiny beam of light that stretches down from the surface of the well. In this deep well metaphor, this light originates from the Sun. The Sun in the picture represents everything in our lives that we are truly grateful for and feel blessed to have. It stands for everything that gives our lives meaning and value.

Radiating from the Sun's rays is *warmth*, which symbolizes the *intensity* of appreciation that we *feel* for our blessings. The intensity of heat radiating from the Sun is *strongest* when positioned at the top of the well. Conversely, its intensity is *weakest* at the bottom of the well, where one treads the Dark Water of Despair. In this place, the only evidence of *good* in the life of someone struggling in this disorder is the tiny beam of sunlight. As indicated, this beam is hardly noticeable when submerged in the Dark Water of Despair. In other words, when you are trapped in that *dark place* in depression, it can be very difficult to appreciate the blessings that exist in your life.

Rope of Support

In the picture above, I would like to draw your attention to the two individuals standing beside the well, holding onto a rope. These individuals symbolize the people in our lives, as well as the resources available, to help us in our disorder. These might be those closest to us, like family members or friends; they could represent health professionals; and so on. The people holding onto the rope represent our network of supporters – and the rope they have gripped tightly in hand serves to symbolize them reaching out to us.

Now draw your attention to the opposite end of the rope, floating at the bottom of the well. It rests along the surface of the water, clearly within reach of the person treading the Dark Water of Despair. The rope serves to symbolize a *support mechanism* with two distinct purposes: firstly, with your supporters holding on tightly, the rope serves as a mechanism to help pull you out of the Dark Water of Despair. Your supporters can pull you up to the first rung on the ladder, away from the relentless attacks by the Piranhas of Depression. Secondly, the rope serves as your safety line to grasp onto at any time when you feel like you may be losing grip of the ladder.

The rope serves as a powerful metaphor in this deep well perspective because its *effectiveness* as a healing agent in depression hinges on a single action: *choice*. That is, when submerged in the Dark Water of Despair, or what is typically referred to in this disorder as that *dark place*, you either choose to reach for the rope, or you choose to <u>not</u> reach for it. I believe that this is a critical first step in healing because until you make the *proactive* and *responsible* choice to reach for the rope, you cannot put your journey to healing in motion.

The conscious *act* of reaching for the rope is symbolic of what I referred to earlier as the *defibrillator* moment in depression. I experienced my defibrillator moment the night my daughter reached out to me, and as deep as I was in that well, it forced me to pull my head out of the water in a whiplash motion, motivating me to reach for the rope with all of my strength. This act served as a crucial first step toward a long and difficult healing process in my disorder. With the rope tightly in hand, my supporters were able to pull me out of the Dark Water of Despair, to a height where I was able to reach the bottom rung on the ladder.

There is a very important limitation, however, with respect to the conceptual Rope of Support: your supporters <u>cannot</u> pull you out of the Deep Well of Depression. In other words, they cannot do the work for you in terms of overcoming depressive symptoms. This can be a considerable cause of frustration for some supporters who may not understand why this person won't simply let them *fix the problem*. I believe that part of the frustration stems from a lack of understanding about the sheer complexity of this disorder.

Here is my perception of why supporters in this deep well context cannot *fix the* problem: the person treading the Dark Water of Despair, oppressed by his depressive symptoms, is tired and worn down by the merciless strikes by the Piranhas of Depression. He may hear his supporters instructing him to hold on to the rope so they can pull him out, but this can be a hopeless endeavor. The person in the well could very well reach for the rope with one hand, but he remains restrained in this disorder so long as he maintains his grip on the Weeds of Damaging Beliefs. This, combined with the relentless attacks by the Piranhas of Depression, renders the person exhausted, both mentally and physically. Even if he could release his grip from the weeds, the person would lack the mental and physical strength to hold onto the rope long enough for his supporters to pull him up to the surface. Without that *defibrillator* moment or the resolve to fight his depressive oppression, the person would eventually succumb to his symptoms. In the figurative context, this means he would let go of the Rope of Support, and plunge back into the Dark Water of Despair.

The Cover

The next feature I would like to draw your attention to in the Deep Well of Depression illustration is the Cover that leans against the opening of the well. Its symbolic significance is simply to remind you that you are never truly trapped in this disorder, even though you may *feel* like you are.

Consider the following rationale: first, think about how you got depressed in the first place. Depression, we have learned, is a disorder of the mind and is not a product of conscious *choice*. Therefore, in the context of the Deep Well of Depression, you do not consciously choose to remove the Cover of the well and jump in. Rather, depression is a mental illness that develops by physiological and psychological means. The opening of the well is never covered, which serves to symbolize that anyone is susceptible to mental illness. Anyone can find themselves treading the Dark Water of Despair at some point in their lives.

Another reason I believe you are never truly trapped in this disorder is because of where your supporters are positioned in this conceptual illustration. Holding onto the rope, they stand by the opening of the well, willing to help you in their respective capacities. No one wants to see you fail in this disorder, so your supporters will always ensure that the opening of the well remains unobstructed – in hopes that you will someday find the strength to overcome your depressive symptoms, and climb out of the well.

61

Ladder of Liberation

The final feature in the Deep Well of Depression illustration is what I call the Ladder of Liberation. Look closely at the illustration above and observe two important characteristics of the ladder: firstly, the ladder is out of reach for the person treading the Dark Water of Despair, and secondly, the ladder has *seven* individual rungs or steps.

Characteristic #1: The ladder is out of reach

In order to access the lowest rung on the Ladder of Liberation, the person must first reach for the Rope of Support floating on the surface of the water. This means that he must consciously *choose* to reach for the rope with both hands – requiring him to release his grip on the Weeds of Damaging Beliefs. Once he has the rope gripped tightly in hand, his supporters can then pull him out of the Dark Water of Despair and up to the first rung on the Ladder of Liberation. I can speak from my own personal experience that this act of gripping onto the Rope of Support is the first *proactive* and *responsible* action step to healing in depression.

I stated above that the supporters in this context cannot pull the person out of the well, meaning they cannot *fix the problem*. His supporters do, however, play two critical roles in the healing journey: firstly, they help the person directly by pulling him up to the first rung on the Ladder of Liberation; and secondly, they provide ongoing support for the person as he progresses in his healing, or as he climbs the ladder. The rope dangling by the ladder serves to symbolize this supporting mechanism. It serves as a safety line that the person can reach for during those times when he may feel like he's losing grip on the ladder at any time throughout his healing process.

Characteristic #2: There are seven (7) rungs on the ladder

The second characteristic of the Ladder of Liberation is that it has a total of seven rungs or steps leading up to the surface of the well. The action of reaching for the rope while treading the Dark Water of Despair is what sets your journey to healing into motion. As described above, your supporters can help in the process by pulling you up to the first ladder rung.

At this point, you hang from the bottom rung on the Ladder of Liberation, arms fully extended. When you look down, you observe below your feet the Dark Water of Despair, and when you look up, you count seven ladder rungs leading to the opening of the well. It is in this moment that you experience *hope* in your disorder, because you are now able to see a way out. The seven ladder rungs (i.e. steps) are labelled as follows:

Step 1: Defibrillate your depression

Step 2: Get help

Step 3: Forgive yourself

Step 4: Create a goal to look forward to

Step 5: Leverage exercise to alleviate depressive symptoms

Step 6: Embrace the good in your life

Step 7: Give back and help others

CHAPTER 4

My 'Deep Well' of Depression

"Can you help me understand why I learned to hate myself?"

This was a question that I had posed to my therapist during a session when we discussed a particular low point in my disorder. I couldn't understand how I got there, why I was feeling the way I was, or how I could regard my life with such indifference. I had no answers, and it was frustrating for me because I'd always prided myself on having a strong aptitude for logical and rational thinking.

I asked my doctor if he could help me understand this, if he could somehow pinpoint a time in my past that may have served to *trigger* what evolved into a state of depression. In my mind, I was convinced that the cause of my disorder was situational in nature, brought on by what I perceived were difficult life events. Indeed, in the decade or so leading up to my diagnosis, I cultivated tremendous guilt and regret about certain life decisions that I had made which I felt produced painful consequences, not only for me but for my family as well. I felt that because I had blamed myself for everything that I perceived *had gone wrong* in my life, that over time, I just grew to hate myself for it.

I explained to my therapist my own interpretation of what it was like for me afflicted with this disorder, using my deep well analogy.

TREADING THE DARK WATER OF DESPAIR

While treading the Dark Water of Despair, I had gripped tightly in hand Weeds of Damaging Beliefs, about myself and those I loved. It felt as though a dark force radiated from my contaminated belief system, communicating to me in what I would describe as a *third-person voice*. I would hear condemning assertions like *I hate myself! I'm worthless!* Most painful: *My family would be better off without me!* This voice intensified the longer my symptoms remained unresolved. It felt that the more condemning it grew, the more convincing it became. This entity, it seemed, controlled my thoughts, which in turn, dictated my emotions.

In my Deep Well of Depression, I felt trapped. There was nowhere to run, nowhere to hide from this disorder. Naked and vulnerable, I felt defenseless to its exploitation. My disorder had become my *master.*

65

In my darkest moments, the master had convinced me of some very terrible things. The most painful was that I was failing my family. It had convinced me that I had nothing more to offer them, and the feeling that I was failing my children crushed me. My master had convinced me that my family was *better off without me* and I knew deep down in my heart that, without them, my life would be meaningless. My master tried to submerge me in the Dark Water of Despair, and it took everything I had to stay afloat. It hurt so much. I just wanted the torment to stop.

I wish I could say that I never contemplated suicide, but this would be untrue. It was a recurring thought over the many months leading up to the night my daughter reached out to me. My master in this disorder was convincing, but deep down, I had enough strength and reason to contemplate the potential consequences that ending my life would produce for my family. These vivid images disturbed me beyond words. I couldn't leave my wife and children to spend the rest of their lives blaming themselves, tormented by questions as to why I would leave them alone in this world.

My biggest leverage preventing me from doing the unthinkable was the thought of igniting a similar depressive episode in any one of my children that could lead them down this tragic path. No matter how much the master tortured me, I knew that I couldn't do that to my family.

Continuing with the deep well metaphor, the most painful of all scars that I had experienced while treading the Dark Water of Despair came from the merciless attacks by the *Family/home* piranha of depression. I had starved this particular piranha because I was convinced that I was failing in my personal relationships, with my extended family as well as my wife and children.

Long before recognizing symptoms of my disorder, I grew increasingly withdrawn from my parents and relatives. I affirmed many times, mostly in thought, that I did not need them in my life, and that they did not need me. I never consciously chose to think this way, but I do remember harboring resentful feelings as far back as I can remember. I had a good upbringing; our household was governed by strong Christian values. My father was the disciplinarian of the family, but he was never too proud to say *I love you*. My mother was the foremost caregiver. But throughout my childhood and into my adult years, I grew bitter.

The resentment that I cultivated toward my family, however, paled in comparison to the magnitude of it I generated toward myself. The years of self-blame for all the perceived wrongs in my life compounded into what I would describe as a negative life force with relentless momentum. I was angry. My master was angry. At times, when I could suppress it, life seemed normal. But when I couldn't, I felt overwhelmed. My perceptions about the world around me, about the people around me, the people that I love, would become distorted.

In this depressive frame, I cultivated limiting beliefs about my marriage and my place in our family unit, anchored by a deficient regard for self-worth. At times, I felt the need to blame others for my conditions. My master was there to induce feelings of resentment and regret toward my marriage, for example, when I was most vulnerable. However, I couldn't communicate these feelings to my wife – my master convinced me not to burden our relationship by communicating my pain. I wasn't able to form the words to verbally express the limiting

67

beliefs, like I was a failure as a husband and a failure as a father to my children. I couldn't bring myself to tell her that I felt she and the kids would be better off without me. I couldn't tell her that I felt I had nothing more to offer her. The master had convinced me that my feelings were insignificant. It made me believe that I was insignificant.

RELATIONSHIPS AND AMBIVALENCE

I discussed in great length with my therapist some very difficult experiences that occurred early in my life. These were experiences that I believed contributed to my difficulty in recognizing self-worth and cultivating healthy relationships. Despite the resentment I had fostered toward my extended family, I affirmed to my doctor that I truly loved them. I valued my friendships that I have built over the years, but my perceived inferiorities made it seemingly impossible to maintain them. And I especially loved my wife, but my master had convinced me to resist confiding in her, my best friend, when I needed her the most.

My therapist explained that this "love-hate" element that exists in relationships is not uncommon because the person that you sometimes *hate* tends to be someone you have an emotional connection to. In other words, you *hate the ones you love*. When you feel resentment or hate toward someone, it is typical for there to exist at the same time an element of attraction, affection, or love for this person. This is the love-hate paradox in a relationship, or in other words, a state of ambivalence. Merriam-Webster Dictionary defines ambivalence as: "simultaneous and contradictory attitudes or feelings (as attraction and repulsion) toward an object, person, or action; and uncertainty as to which approach to follow."

THE "BITTER DIVIDE" OF AMBIVALENCE

While treading the Dark Water of Despair in my mental disorder, I believed that I was trapped in what I would describe as a *bitter divide* of ambivalence with respect to my relationships. I was angry and felt a great deal of resentment, and at times hatred, towards the very people in my life that, by contradiction, I loved deep down. Convinced, I told my doctor that I believed it came down to a choice: you either choose to love or you choose to hate. In between is uncertainty and bitterness.

SEARCHING FOR THE ANSWER

I discussed with my therapist some very difficult life experiences throughout the many months of counseling. I shared my perceptions and beliefs that I had formed from these experiences. My view of the world around me, my relationships, was trapped in what I believed was a bitter divide of ambivalence. The bitterness and uncertainty in this place generated a great deal of frustration in my life. With Weeds of Damaging Beliefs gripped tightly in hand, I was submerged in my disorder.

I couldn't understand why I felt the way I did, nor could I rationalize this dark place that I was in psychologically. I yearned for an answer - I needed to know. So I asked my therapist if he could help me find *the answer.*

He explained that to find this so-called answer or trigger I was looking for would be like trying to find a needle in a haystack, providing it even existed. However, he did make three fundamental observations with respect to my disorder. The meaning behind the cliché *be careful what you*

69

wish for, you just may get it was never more apparent to me until one particular session when my therapist found what I perceived were the missing puzzle pieces. I was unprepared for what came next, and as for that Deep Well of Depression, it became all too clear why I was there.

I refer to his observations as *discoveries*, because when my therapist shared them with me, they shattered everything I thought I knew about my life, my relationships, and especially, my disorder.

The first discovery was how I was interpreting human value or self-worth; the second was my limiting interpretation of *ambivalence* with respect to my personal relationships; and the third, one that I would identify was the *needle* in the haystack I was looking for, was that I was *terrified of my anger.*

Discovery #1: On Human Value

My therapist indicated that part of the deficiency with respect to my disorder lay in how I was interpreting *human value,* or more specifically, how I perceived *self-worth.* He referred to an important statement that I had made in an earlier session when talking about my father. I said that I admired him because no matter how difficult life got, he always had faith and managed to find happiness during the worst of times. I admired this trait in him because, by comparison, I couldn't do that. It was a struggle for me to find value in myself during life's challenges. I lacked faith of any kind and failed to recognize the silver lining when overshadowed by a dark cloud. Instead, I would break myself down by constantly blaming myself and my conditions. This made it difficult for me to deal with my challenges – and even more difficult to be the father, husband and man that I perceived my family needed me to be.

He explained that both my father and I had conflicting interpretations of human value: my father's was value-based while mine was conditional on meeting certain expectations that I established for myself. I realized in my healing that throughout my childhood and right up into my adult years, I consistently failed to meet the perceived *criteria* I set for myself to be a person *worthy* of value.

I also came to realize that the criteria I set for myself were out of reach. Because of this, I failed consistently to live up to my own expectations. I found it hard to accept who I was and it was difficult for me to acknowledge any good that I would accomplish in my life because I was too focused on my perceived failures. When my spirits were raised, it would only take a pinch of adversity to deflate any perspective of good in my life.

I realized only after having suffered in my disorder that my father had it right all along. He *chose* to find happiness in the worst of circumstances because he placed at the forefront of everything the very things he valued in his life: God, family and relationships. He did not perceive himself as a failure to his family during hardship, but rather, he saw himself as a man who was not going to give up on his family when times get difficult, under any circumstances. From this, he found purpose, and this is how he could look us in the eye and feel proud because no matter what, he was going to be there to protect us. He discovered value in his suffering and faith in his God.

Discovery #2: On Ambivalence

My doctor challenged me in my belief about relationships and ambivalence when I said: *you either choose to love or you choose to hate, and in between is uncertainty and bitterness.* He explained that it is human nature to exist from time to time within this divide, between love and hate, because it is in this place where we cultivate relationships.

Anger, resentment and hatred are natural human emotions, as are happiness, attraction and love. This is why it is okay to experience resentment toward someone you love, so long as these feelings are processed in a *healthy way* – that is, through *communication*. Emotions like anger or disappointment can be reconciled when communicated effectively, but in the absence of open communication, such emotions can stew, and grow out of proportion.

To illustrate, my doctor shared a time when he experienced resentful feelings toward his teenage daughter for something that she had done. He began to ignore her, giving her the cold shoulder treatment for some time. He could sense her discomfort when they were in the same room together and when he finally approached her and shared his feelings about the thing that upset him in the first place, she was overcome with relief. She finally understood why their relationship was temporarily strained. She wasn't so much bothered by the specific thing that upset her father, but rather, she was more troubled by why he was acting the way he was.

My doctor emphasized from this example that for his daughter, the pain of *not knowing* was far greater than the pain of *knowing* because with the latter, there is understanding and truth. He explained that because of this experience, he and his daughter were able to resolve their conflict and by the process of reconciliation, their relationship grew stronger as a result.

The "healthy divide" of ambivalence

Through therapy and self-reflection, I developed a greater understanding about this concept of ambivalence in relationships. I illustrated my interpretation of ambivalence in the form of a picture (displayed on the next page), recognizing there is no such thing as a *bitter divide*, but rather, a *healthy divide* in ambivalence. I used the metaphor of a river to illustrate my perspective:

River of Relationship Ambivalence

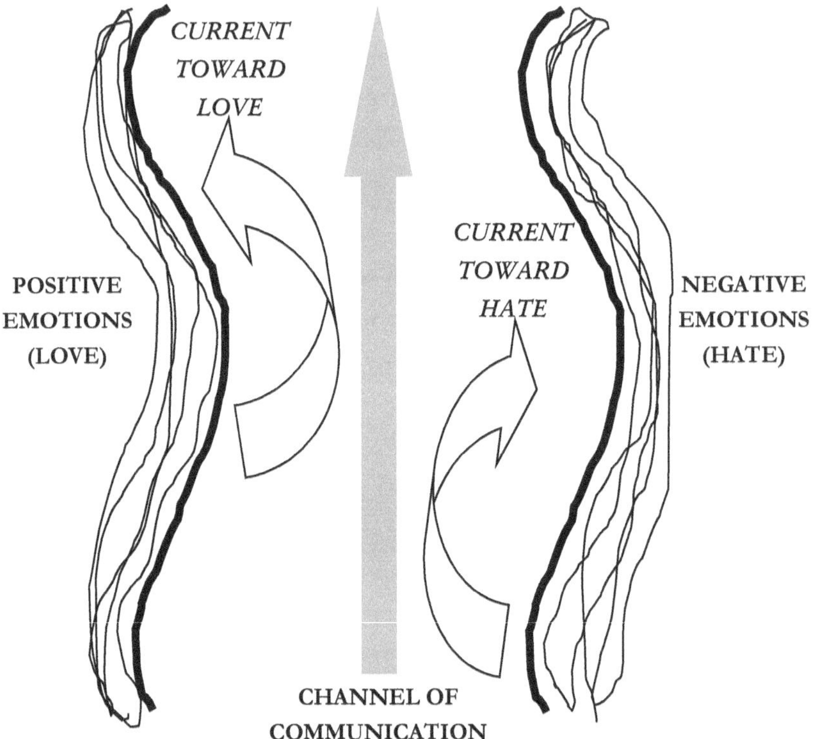

This illustrates that in any relationship, it is okay or healthy to experience conflicting feelings toward someone: positive (such as acceptance, attraction and love) and negative (such as anger, resentment and, though harsh, hatred). The diagram shows two currents: one that pulls our emotions toward the positive (love) shoreline of a relationship and the other that pulls our emotions toward the negative (hate) shoreline. These respective currents represent those times in a relationship when one says or does something that stimulates an emotional response (positive or negative) in the other person.

It is important to note that the force of the current is not influenced by conscious thought, but rather, represents that *unprocessed*, initial gut-feeling stimulated by how the other person's actions were perceived.

The final feature of the ambivalent river shown in the diagram is the Channel of Communication. I have learned through discussions with my therapist that this channel is where relationships can thrive and grow.

There are times that the current will pull us out of the channel and toward the negative shoreline, and there will be times when things are going great in a relationship, and we gravitate toward the positive shoreline. As wonderful as it would be to stay on this positive shoreline forever, it is not, for all intents and purposes, feasible.

When the negative current pulls you out of the Channel of Communication, or the state of contentment in a relationship, and toward the Shoreline of Negative Emotions, the health of a relationship is vulnerable. I have learned in my own experience that the longer we tread water against the current along the negative shoreline, the harder it is to swim back to the Channel of Communication. This is representative of growing tired and worn in a relationship. I believe that when we quit, or choose to stop swimming against the current, relationships ultimately fail.

However, when you put everything you've got into a relationship – that is, when you choose to fight the current and strive for the Channel of Communication, relationships can grow stronger and more fruitful. I believe that it is in this place where we can leverage the power of communication to weaken the current that pulls us toward the negative shoreline. A powerful and positive consequence from this is that

75

relationships stand to grow stronger and more resilient during trying times.

During our discussion, my therapist explained that the most productive thing I could have done to weaken the negative current in my marriage was to tell my wife exactly how I felt. In this scenario, she would have had the opportunity to learn the truth about how I was feeling and why I was growing so distant and cold in our relationship.

By affording her this truth, she then could have processed my emotions while re-evaluating her own beliefs with respect to our relationship. By working together, communicating, we would have been better positioned to reconcile our differences and ultimately, strengthen our relationship.

During these challenging times, however, I didn't communicate my feelings with her. The current that pulled me toward the Shoreline of Negative Emotions, I felt, grew stronger. Or I became weaker. It wasn't until my doctor made the third discovery in my disorder when I realized why I didn't communicate my feelings: *it was because I couldn't.*

Discovery #3: On Anger

My therapist broke ground into the core of my mental disorder when we delved deep into some difficult childhood experiences and analyzed their effect on my emotional development over time. But it was his next statement that shattered everything I thought I had known about my life and especially, my disorder. He said: *I believe that you have grown to be terrified of your anger.*

I didn't understand it. My mind was scrambling, trying to make sense of his words. But I couldn't, and this generated a great deal of frustration. I became overwhelmed in emotion because everything that I had believed up to this point about my mental erosion, and eventual plummet into the Deep Well of Depression, was now in question. My personal beliefs were unexpectedly blindsided by a single, conflicting medical opinion.

My doctor sensed my discomfort and began walking me through it, to help piece the puzzle together so I could see it for myself. He began by emphasizing that throughout our discussions I would momentarily expose uncomfortable feelings of resentment and anger with respect to my personal relationships, but then would instantly retract and suppress them. I would replace them with expressions of love and acceptance, carefully rationalized, in an attempt to drive back those negative emotions and my shame for feeling them. Where I should have addressed and communicated such difficult feelings, and allowed for reconciliation, instead I suppressed and internalized them.

My doctor helped me recognize that by burying my true feelings and emotions, I stood to contaminate my mental landscape. Contaminated

77

soil then produces contaminated crops (i.e. beliefs). He explained that unless we learn to filter out these contaminants, our belief systems become vulnerable to breakdown and decay.

This realization, I believe, proved to be the turning point in my therapy. My doctor pinpointed what I considered was the root cause of my mental disorder: *I lacked the ability to express confrontational emotions toward other people due to my fear of anger.* Instead, I conditioned myself from an early age to suppress and filter them, inward and toward myself.

He asked me a question which served as the final nail in the coffin, so to speak. He asked if I had ever fought with my wife. I told him that I didn't remember ever having fought or yelled at her. I couldn't remember the last time I engaged in a heated discussion with anyone for that matter. Upon reflection, anytime I would be exposed to a confrontational or uncomfortable situation that involved feeling angry or frustrated, the only way I knew how to process it was to filter it inward. My doctor explained that although this type of inward filtration can be considered a form of release, it was a very unhealthy one. As for my wife, it became all too clear why her many attempts to reach out to me during the low points in my disorder were unsuccessful. She couldn't reach me because I *couldn't* allow anyone in. What neither of us realized was that I had what I would describe as an *emotional disability,* in that I lacked the ability to effectively function in difficult and confrontational environments.

HURTING THE ONES YOU LOVE

I failed to recognize in my *emotional disability* how much I was hurting the ones I loved. For my wife, she longed for the truth, an answer as to why I was so unhappy in my life. My inability to communicate negative feelings left her with unanswered questions and the endless torment of trying to answer for the both of us what was wrong in our relationship.

With respect to my children, my therapist helped me understand that when my daughter approached me and asked that powerful question: "When you get better, can you build a snowman with me?" what she was really saying was, *Daddy, you are not there for me and this hurts me and I want you to stop hurting me.* My children knew there was something wrong but they didn't know what it was and this was because I couldn't communicate it. They were hurting because they knew I was hurting, but didn't know why.

With respect to my extended family, I struggled for a very long time with conflicting emotions: on one side, I justified my resentment, and on the other side, I justified my love for them. Throughout my life, I harbored these conflicting feelings in what I now know was an ill-conceived notion of ambivalence.

I told my therapist that my father never knew how I felt and that he died with a *broken* son. My doctor explained that because I deprived my father of the truth – about why I remained distant in our relationship – he likely would have suffered more as a result. His long-term suffering from *not knowing* would have been far worse than the short-term pain from learning the truth.

MY PRICE FOR FREEDOM

In the book, *On Ambivalence: The Problems and Pleasures of Having It Both Ways*, the author states that ambivalence "…is a condition worse than most because it can lead to catastrophe…Making a choice gives one a fifty percent chance of being right. Ambivalence would seem to give one a one hundred percent chance of losing out."[9]

One of the most painful realities of discovering the *truth* about my mental disorder was *losing out* what could have otherwise been a prosperous relationship with my father. As difficult as this is to admit, I felt justified at times to stand and watch my father's health deteriorate in the fifteen years leading to his death. I think about some of the things that I would say to myself regarding his ailing health: *He's old enough to know better! If he doesn't want to take care of his health, it's his choice! It's just a matter of time!*

These comments, I have since learned, were generated by what I described earlier as my *master*. Mentally, I was a slave. I listened to the master, and I believed him. Because of this, I was able to walk into my father's wake and suppress my sorrow. When I delivered the eulogy, my true self was briefly exposed from the barriers of oppression as I wept during my speech. But my master was relentless, convincing me that my tears were superficial – inspired only by the sadness and sorrow of the surrounding atmosphere in the church.

But now, I feel that I am the one who has to pay the ultimate price for my mental freedom. My therapist explained that tragically, I deprived my father of an opportunity to reconcile what otherwise could be described as a contaminated relationship between a father and son. I now must accept that this opportunity is forever entombed with the ashes of my late father.

Even more tragic was the realization that I was heading down the very same pathway with my own family, without consciously realizing it. I risked *losing out* with them as I did with my father. And if this had continued, I would have had nothing left in my life to live for. This realization disturbed me greatly because I could see it and could parallel the logic. My belief system was so contaminated that I believed my family would be better off without me. So in the dark depths of my well of depression, I gradually grew more and more withdrawn from the family unit. I failed to recognize that I was hurting my family by surrendering to this depressive, gravitational pull.

CHAPTER 5

Introducing the Powerful Message of Viktor E. Frankl

"Between stimulus and response there is a space. In that space is our power to choose our response. In our response lies our growth and our freedom." – Unknown[10]

INTRODUCING VIKTOR E. FRANKL

Viktor Emil Frankl was a Jewish psychiatrist who was imprisoned in a number of concentration camps – including the infamous Auschwitz death camp – during the Second World War. Frankl was an eyewitness to the most hideous crimes against humanity under the Nazi regime. In his book, *Man's Search for Meaning,* Frankl offers his autobiographical account of his experiences living in concentration camps, and in his work, explores the question of how everyday life in a concentration camp was reflected in the mind of the average prisoner. In his writing, Frankl focused less on the "great horrors" of his experiences but rather, documented "the multitude of small torments" that he and so many prisoners endured in captivity.[11]

THE 'WHY?'

What does Frankl's work have to do with learning to overcome symptoms of depression? I believe: *Everything.* Revisit the opening quote above and pay extra attention to the second sentence: "In that space is our power to choose our response." This *power to choose* how we respond to life's challenges is, in my opinion, the single most fundamental principle that we must leverage before we can truly heal in depression. This serves as the backbone to my Deep Well Perspective Healing approach.

I believe that before we can effectively leverage this power in our healing process, it is critical to first recognize and appreciate the underlying context behind the 'power to choose' principle. It was during his incarceration in a concentration camp that Frankl discovered this principle – that he possessed a fundamental freedom not even his Nazi

83

captives could take away from him: "the freedom to choose one's attitude in any given set of circumstances, to choose one's own way."[12]

Frankl realized and applied this liberating principle under extreme psychic and physical stress. My question is: why can't we leverage this very principle in our own incarceration inside the Deep Well of Depression? There is nothing I could write that could come anywhere near the level of emotional, physical and spiritual suffering that Frankl and the millions of prisoners endured under the Nazi regime. But I do believe it is important to learn about Frankl's account of the multitude of small torments and the lessons learned about human will, or the *last of the human freedoms*, under extraordinary conditions.

The purpose of this exercise is two-fold: firstly, to extract the fundamental principles from Frankl's experiences to which he owed his survival and liberation. These will serve as the very principles that we can apply to our own mental incarceration. Secondly, to establish a *standard for suffering* against which we can measure our own perspective of suffering in depression.

History dictates the horrors of what went on in Nazi death camps throughout World War II. When you are a victim of major depressive disorder, you too feel oppressed like a prisoner – trapped inside a deep well. But our incarceration is figurative in context while Frankl's living hell was real. The pain and suffering that I experienced throughout my mental *solitary confinement* did not appear so terrible after having read what Frankl (and other prisoners in those times) had to endure in their *hell on earth*.

The extent of our physical, emotional and spiritual suffering on an individual basis is relative, and unless we have something to compare it to, we may perceive our suffering to be much larger than it truly is – perhaps even larger than life itself. This is a dangerous mental state. It is a place where we begin to contemplate and question our reason for living. When your personal suffering so consumes you that you fail to acknowledge that things could be worse, I believe you become truly vulnerable.

It is in this place that you need to acknowledge you have the ability to change what you are going through in your life. Although you may not realize this yet, you have the power to make it better. It is in this place that you truly need to appreciate that "…between stimulus and response there is a space. In that space is our power to choose our response. In our response lies our growth and our freedom."[13] It is in this place that you need to acknowledge there is hope for a better tomorrow, should you decide to use your power of choice. It is in this place that you need to understand: *things could be so much worse.* If you struggle to acknowledge this, then please, read on about Viktor E. Frankl's account of life in Nazi death camps.

The following provides a brief timeline leading up to Frankl's arrest:

1938: Hitler invades Austria.

1940-42: Frankl obtains an immigration visa to America but lets it expire because he does not want to desert his aging parents.

1941: Frankl marries his first wife.

1942: the Nazis force Frankl and his wife to abort their baby, and in September of that year, both are arrested along with his parents, and are deported to a concentration camp.

(Source: Viktor Frankl Institute. Retrieved from https://www.viktorfrankl.org)

85

A JOURNEY IN TIME

Stop for a moment and reflect on what you have just read. We need to take the time and emotionally immerse ourselves in what truly was a frightening reality for millions of people in that era. Imagine coming home from work one night to learn that your country was invaded and successfully claimed by an extremist regime. Imagine learning that the freedoms you had previously enjoyed and had taken for granted no longer apply to you.

According to the Viktor Frankl Institute, this extremist regime forced the young couple to abort their baby. I don't know the specific details of what happened, but I can't help but lose myself in the unthinkable tragedy of this life event. Reflect on this for a moment: try to imagine how it must have felt when Frankl and his pregnant wife received a visit from officers of the Third Reich. Think about the shock they must have endured seconds after learning that their pregnancy was in strict violation of *Nazi values*, and that they were required to *kill* their unborn child. Imagine how they must have felt walking into the hospital, stripped of their rights and dignities, sitting in the hospital room and waiting for the doctor to come and abort their baby. Try to envision in your mind the devastation felt by Frankl's wife lying there as the doctor begins the procedure. Now envision Frankl himself, sitting outside the room, waiting helplessly. Look at their faces. Can you envision the pain and suffering both must have endured in that experience?

If you have children, imagine being denied of them, and imagine not having any control over it. How does this make you feel? Does your stomach turn in disgust in response to the anger, hopelessness and despair you might feel? Words could not explain how devastating this experience must have been for Frankl and his wife. Play the movie in your head, put yourself in their shoes and allow this reflection exercise to grip you emotionally. This was a reality for them.

Frankl's Account of His Deportation to Auschwitz

(Selected passages from his book: *A Man's Search For Meaning*)

"Fifteen hundred captives had been travelling by train for several days and nights…Suddenly, a cry broke from the ranks of the anxious passengers, "There is a sign, Auschwitz!"…the very name stood for all that was horrible: gas chambers, crematoriums, massacres…we were cold and hungry…one five-ounce piece of bread was our only food in four days."

"We did not realize the meaning behind the scene that was to follow presently. We were told…to fall into two lines – women on one side, men on the other – in order to file past a senior SS officer…His right hand was lifted, and with the forefinger of that hand he pointed very leisurely to the right or to the left…It was my turn…The SS man looked me over, appeared to hesitate, then put both his hands on my shoulders…and he turned my shoulders very slowly until I faced right, and I moved over to that side."[14]

The picture on the next page (as well as the others that follow in this chapter) comes from the United States Holocaust Memorial Museum (USHMM). This particular photo depicts thousands of people that had just arrived by train at the Auschwitz extermination camp in Poland in 1944. Upon arrival, the Jewish passengers were *selected* by senior officers to stand in one of two lines, the *left* or the *right*. In the distance, you can observe the entrance tower leading into the Auschwitz camp.

A transport of Hungarian Jews lines up for selection at the Auschwitz extermination camp. Poland, May 1944. — Yad Vashem Photo Archives

"The significance of the finger game was explained to us in the evening…it was the first selection…made on our existence or non-existence…For the great majority, it meant death…Their sentence was carried out within the next few hours."[15]

Hungarian Jews on their way to the gas chambers. Auschwitz-Birkenau, Poland, May 1944.— Yad Vashem Photo Archives

The people in this photograph, comprised mostly of women and children, were selected for extermination. In this still frame of time, these human beings were being led to killing centers established by the Nazis for efficient mass murder. Look closely at this photo and observe their faces. Look at the frown of one mother holding her baby. Observe the look of fear and concern on the little boys' faces – and especially the little girl walking behind them. Imagine being there in that line. Imagine what that must have felt like. Imagine that only a few short minutes after this picture was taken, these same persons were fighting for their last breaths in a gas chamber. That baby in the photograph was fighting for his last breath. A baby.

How does this make you feel when you envision yourself there, observing them as they march toward their unknown fate? Imagine the father of one of these children who would have been separated from his family after having been selected for the right line. Imagine the pain and suffering he must have endured thinking about them throughout his incarceration, wondering where they were and how they were being treated. Then think about learning years later the brutal reality that his wife and child were *gassed* just minutes after having been separated from him. It is heart wrenching to look at this photograph. It saddens me to observe their faces and disturbs me to think that at that still frame in time, they had no idea where they were heading as they marched toward the camp. But we know. We know what their fate was just moments after that photographer captured their fearful expressions.

Auschwitz was the largest killing center according to the USHMM, and it is said that at the peak of the deportations to that camp, up to six thousand Jews were gassed each day. Frankl writes about the fate of those people who were selected to stand in the *left* line:

"For the great majority of our transport, about 90 percent, it meant death…Those who were sent to the left were marched from the (train) station straight to the crematorium. This building, as I was told by someone who worked there had the word "bath" written over its doors…On entering, each prisoner was handed a piece of soap, and then-but mercifully I do not need to describe the events which followed."[16]

They were deceived into thinking that the room (pictured on the next page) was a showering facility. Its true identity was that of a gas chamber and this served as the final destination for millions of people – of fathers, mothers, and children.

Gas chamber in the main camp of Auschwitz immediately after liberation. Poland, January 1945 — Dokumentationsarchiv des Oesterreichischen Widerstandes.

Frankl's personal accounts and observations
of life in Nazi death camps

The following are selected passages from Frankl's book which intimately describes his experiences living in concentration camps:

"Next we were herded into another room to be shaved…not a hair was left on our entire bodies…our nakedness was brought home to us…all we possessed, literally, was our naked existence."

"The thought of suicide was entertained by nearly everyone…It was born of the hopelessness of the situation, the constant danger of death looming over us daily and hourly, and the closeness of the deaths suffered by many of the others."

"Apathy…eventually made him insensitive to daily and hourly beatings."

"Reality dimmed, and all efforts and all emotions were centered on one task: preserving one's own life and that of the other fellow."

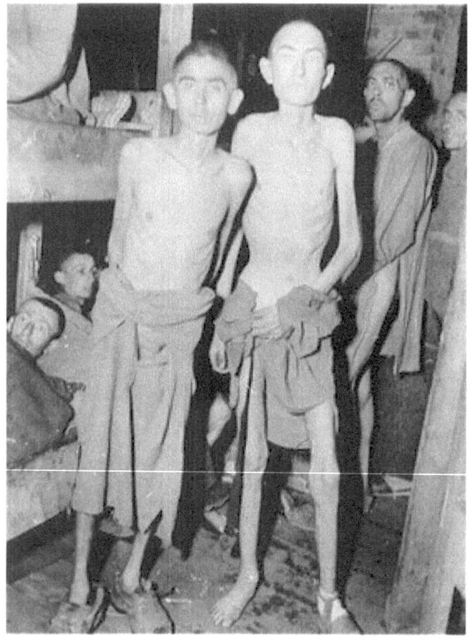

"When the last layers of subcutaneous fat had vanished, and we looked like skeletons disguised with skin and rags, we could watch our bodies beginning to devour themselves. The organism digested its own protein, and the muscles disappeared."[17]

Survivors of the Ampfing subcamp of the Dachau concentration camp soon after liberation by US troops. Ampfing, Germany, May 4, 1945.
— National Archives and Records Administration, College Park, Md.

Frankl's Spiritual Awakening: His Words

"In spite of all the enforced physical and mental primitiveness of the life in a concentration camp, it was possible for spiritual life to deepen…Let me tell you what happened on those early mornings when we had to march to our work site.

We stumbled on in the darkness, over big stones and through large puddles, along the one road leading from the camp. The accompanying guards kept shouting at us and driving us with the butts of their rifles. Anyone with very sore feet supported himself on his neighbor's arm. Hardly a word was spoken; the icy wind did not encourage talk. Hiding his mouth behind his upturned collar, the man marching next to me whispered suddenly: 'If our wives could see us now! I do hope they are better off in their camps and don't know what is happening to us.'

That brought thoughts of my own wife to mind. And as we stumbled on for miles, slipping on icy spots, supporting each other time and again, dragging one another up and onward, nothing was said, but we both knew: each of us was thinking of his wife…my mind clung to my wife's image, imagining it with an uncanny acuteness. I heard her answering me, saw her smile, her frank and encouraging look. Real or not, her look was then more luminous than the sun which was beginning to rise.

A thought transfixed me: for the first time in my life I saw the truth… that love is the ultimate and the highest goal to which man can aspire. Then I grasped the meaning of the greatest secret that human poetry and human thought and belief have to impart: *The salvation of man is through love and in love.* I understood how a man who has nothing left in this world still may know bliss…in the contemplation of his beloved. In a position of utter desolation, when man cannot express himself in positive action…in such a position man can, through loving contemplation of the image he carries of his beloved, achieve fulfillment."[18]

CHAPTER 6

'Choice' – The Impetus for Change

Viktor Frankl's account of prison life in Nazi concentration camps provides an unparalleled standard of human suffering that is incredibly difficult to fathom. Between 1942 and 1945, Frankl lost everything in his life. He lost his career, his unborn child, his wife, his mother (who was murdered in the gas chamber), and his father (who died of exhaustion/starvation). He was imprisoned in four separate death camps and existed in the absence of any constitutional rights and freedoms for nearly three years. The man witnessed and experienced unimaginable human suffering.

In the same context of the Piranhas of Depression, virtually every area of his life was inflicted with pain and suffering. Clearly, Viktor Frankl had plenty of reasons to plunge into the Deep Well of Depression and submerge his head under the dark water, surrendering to each successive bite from the merciless fish. He had every reason to give up. This in my mind would have been the inevitable fate of any person subject to such horrors. Who would have blamed him for sparing himself further misery? But as it turned out, Viktor Frankl chose instead to embrace meaning in his life - to give himself a reason to survive, something to look forward to, a reason to keep fighting. He chose instead to find meaning in his suffering.

Frankl battled against extreme mental anguish throughout his ordeal because he preserved what he referred to as "the last of the human freedoms," the one and only thing that he possessed that not even his Nazi captives could take away from him: the freedom "to choose one's attitude in any given set of circumstances, to choose one's own way."[19]

According to Frankl, a person "...*can* preserve a vestige of spiritual freedom, of independence of mind, even in such terrible conditions of psychic and physical stress."[20]

This is an extraordinary message in and of itself. Notice that the word *can* is in italics. This suggests that human beings have the ability to preserve independence of mind regardless of how bad things get in their lives, should they *choose* to do so.

Frankl describes this affirmation with personal experience: "We who lived in concentration camps can remember the men who walked through the huts comforting others, giving away their last piece of bread. They may have been few in number, but they offer sufficient proof that everything can be taken from a man but...the last of the human freedoms..."[21]

LAST OF THE HUMAN FREEDOMS

The *last of the human freedoms* was a fundamental principle of Frankl's attitude and ultimate survival throughout his incarceration in Nazi concentration camps during World War II. Frankl identified two other principles which he believed were essential to a prisoner's defenses against the camps' *psychopathological influences*: the first involved finding meaning in one's life (and in one's suffering), and the second, finding a future goal to look forward to.

When collectively applied to the concept of the Deep Well of Depression, I believe that these three principles offer tremendous leverage in overcoming debilitating symptoms. These principles are qualified below by Frankl's own words - supported by his experiences and interpretations of how these principles influenced prisoner life in concentration camps. In addition, I make the intuitive connection to depression in the context of how we can apply these principles to overcome depressive symptoms.

Principle #1: You Have the Power to Choose

"…I may give the impression that the human being is completely and unavoidably influenced by his surroundings. But what about human liberty? Is that theory true which would have us believe that man is no more than a product of many conditional and environmental factors - be they of a biological, psychological or sociological nature?…We can answer these questions from experience as well as on principle. The experiences of camp life show that man does have a choice of action. There were enough examples…which proved that apathy could be overcome, irritability suppressed."[22]

The *last of the human freedoms* is the freedom to choose how we respond to any given set of circumstances in our lives. This parallels the 'power to choose' principle introduced in the opening quote of Chapter 5. These words offer a deep and powerful meaning which, I believe, we must learn to fully embrace. Further, I believe that there must be a genuine desire to discover it for oneself, especially when feeling oppressed by depressive symptoms. There are two facets underlying the intrinsic meaning of the 'power to choose' principle which I believe we must learn to come to terms with before we can begin to climb the Ladder of Liberation.

The first is accepting that we have the power to choose how we respond to life's questions, or challenges; and the second, accepting that your attitude toward life's challenges is a matter of *inner decision* and not a matter of your external environment. I believe that the first step toward overcoming depressive symptoms is to unconditionally embrace the *last of the human freedoms* principle.

Principle #2: Find Meaning in Your Life and in Your Suffering

"We must never forget that we may also find meaning in life even when confronted with a hopeless situation, when facing a fate that cannot be changed. For what then matters is to bear witness to the uniquely human potential at its best, which is to transform a personal tragedy into a triumph, to turn one's predicament into a human achievement…In some way, suffering ceases to be suffering at the moment it finds a meaning, such as the meaning of a sacrifice."[23]

Frankl identified three ways in which human beings can discover meaning in their lives:

(1) by striving to achieve or accomplish a goal;

(2) by inspiring one's soul with the beauty or truth or love for something (art or culture) or someone (spouse or child);

(3) by discovering in oneself an opportunity to find meaning in unavoidable suffering.

Frankl found meaning in both his life and his suffering during his imprisonment. He realized that a man who has lost everything could still achieve fulfillment (and meaning) by envisioning someone whom he deeply loved (i.e. his wife). After having been infected with typhus, Frankl began to reconstruct his manuscript, which he had lost soon after his deportation. He did so in order to stay alert and avoid delirium. In this project, he was able to find meaning.

On suffering, Frankl indicated that nobody wanted to die for nothing and for him, religious faith provided meaning in his suffering. He spoke of a fellow prisoner who made a pact with God that his suffering and

99

death should serve to save the life of a loved one. In his pact, the prisoner was able to find meaning in his sacrifice.

As I mentioned earlier, depression is a catalyst for *hopelessness*, which means *having no expectation of good or success*. "Having no expectation" could also imply *lacking any significance*, which is a definition for the word *meaningless*. It stands to reason than in order to effectively counter the feeling of hopelessness, one must discover meaning in one's own life. This, I believe, serves as a precursor to overcoming depressive symptoms.

Principle #3: Find a Future Goal to Look Forward To

"Almost in tears from pain (…I had terrible sores on my feet from wearing torn shoes), I limped a few kilometers…to our work site. Very cold, bitter winds struck us. I kept thinking of the endless little problems of our miserable life…I became disgusted with the state of affairs which compelled me, daily and hourly, to think of only such trivial things. I forced my thoughts to turn to another subject. Suddenly I saw myself standing on the platform of a well-lit, warm and pleasant lecture room. In front of me sat an attentive audience on comfortable upholstered seats. I was giving a lecture on the psychology of the concentration camp.…By this method I succeeded somehow in rising above the situation, above the sufferings of the moment, and I observed them as if they were already in the past."[24]

On life in the concentration camps, Frankl spoke of the inherent dangers that surrounded inmates who preferred to live in the past as a means of making their present horrors less of a reality. In this instance, he indicated that prisoners deprived themselves of the opportunities to learn and grow from their present difficulties, and neglected to accept the camps' challenges as a test of inner strength or a test of faith. Instead, they chose to live in the past, absent of a future goal, and life for them, Frankl describes, became *meaningless.*

The principle of finding a future goal to look forward to instills *purpose* in a person's life and provides a reason to move forward, or in the context of the Deep Well of Depression, to climb. With purpose, a person struggling in this disorder can find within themselves the will to survive and a desire to learn and grow from a difficult situation.

TAKING RESPONSIBILITY

I was first exposed to Frankl's freedom to choose principle in the book: *"The Seven Habits of Highly Effective People,"* by Stephen R. Covey[25]. I immersed myself in Covey's interpretation of this principle and adopted the reality that I, myself, was ultimately responsible for my own life. This meant that I am where I am today because of the choices I had made in the past.

The difficult part in accepting these ideals, however, was that I had to stop blaming other people, and my conditions, for my circumstances. I had to assume complete and unconditional ownership of my life. Initially, I understood this, and respected Covey's interpretations, but lacked conviction in the principle. Covey indicates in his book that it is, in fact, a very hard concept to accept, emotionally.

I knew that if I was to have any success in influencing change within myself and my disorder, I needed conviction in my belief of the *freedom to choose* principle and everything it stands for. I yearned for an emotional

101

grip on this principle which led me to Frankl's book, *Man's Search For Meaning*[26]. When I read it, learning intimately about the real and horrific circumstances upon which this principle is based, I discovered my conviction. I no longer accepted excuses for my suffering and blocked out any sign of defeatism that would otherwise serve to oppress my spirit.

I made the conscious *choice* to fight against the oppressive symptoms of my depression by applying the fundamental principles presented in this chapter. This enabled me to discover meaning in my life and in my suffering; and by creating goals to look forward to, I gained the strength and momentum to successfully climb out of the Deep Well of Depression.

My sincere hope at this point is that you not only recognize the importance of leveraging these very principles in your own life, but you find conviction in them. I personally believe that the key to successfully healing in depression lies in the principles rooted in the *last of the human freedoms*.

CHAPTER 7

The 'Proactive – Liberation Model' for Depression

I have come to realize throughout my struggle with depression that the *last of the human freedoms* principle, that is, the belief that we are free to choose how we respond to life's challenges, must not only be acknowledged, but accepted, before we can truly heal in this disorder. Accepting this was one of the most difficult steps in my healing process because it forced me to embrace a new series of beliefs while laying some old, limiting beliefs to rest. For example, I learned to accept the following beliefs – which I call, *liberating* beliefs:

103

Liberating beliefs:

I am responsible for my own life.

I am free to choose how I respond to life's challenges.

The most difficult challenge at this stage of healing is to not only adopt these beliefs, but to reject the following *limiting* beliefs:

Limiting beliefs:

I am determined by my conditions.

I am determined by my conditioning.

I firmly believe that liberation from major depressive symptoms is not achievable unless we choose to replace *limiting* beliefs with *liberating* beliefs. To do this, we have to adopt a proactive state of thinking.

PROACTIVE VERSUS REACTIVE

In his book *The Seven Habits of Highly Effective People*, Covey distinguishes between proactive and reactive people as follows:

"Look at the word responsibility – "response-ability" – the ability to choose your response. Highly proactive people recognize that responsibility. They do not blame circumstances, conditions, or conditioning for their behavior. Their behavior is a product of their own conscious choice, based on values, rather than a product of their conditions, based on feeling."[27]

"Reactive people are often affected by their physical environment. If the weather is good, they feel good. If it isn't, it affects their attitude…Reactive people are also affected by their social environment…When people treat them well, they feel well; when people don't, they become defensive…Reactive people are driven by feelings, by circumstances, by conditions, by their environment."[28]

The underlying message is that we have the choice to empower ourselves (to be the master) or empower our conditions (to be the slave) under any given set of circumstances. Frankl's story is a testament to the power of choice, the conscious ability to choose value-based responses under the most horrific of circumstances. Covey states: "The ability to subordinate an impulse to a value is the essence of the proactive person."[29]

To echo Covey's words, we have the ability – the power of choice – to rewrite new programs, or belief systems, for ourselves, fully apart from our personal conditions and conditioning. For example, the power of choice makes the difference in children of alcoholic parents, between those who will repeat their parents' fate and those who will not. It's an all too familiar story: *He's an alcoholic because his father is an alcoholic.* But also common: *He's __not__ an alcoholic because his father is an alcoholic.*

So the question is: How do we rewrite a new belief system after years of conditioning and fostering of *limiting* beliefs? How do we become *proactive* in our thinking? Covey explains that "…proactive people are driven by values – carefully thought about, selected and internalized values."[30] According to Covey, their behavior, or how they respond, is a product of conscious choice. Choices too can be carefully thought about, selected and internalized. This serves as the foundation for Covey's "Proactive Model", which is illustrated on the next page:

105

Covey's "Proactive Model"

STIMULUS ⟹ FREEDOM TO CHOOSE ⟹ RESPONSE

- Self-awareness
- Imagination
- Conscience
- Independent Will

Source: *The 7 Habits of Highly Effective People: Powerful Lessons in Personal Change.* Covey, Stephen R

Covey explains that how we choose to respond to a particular stimulus or action is formed from the following *human endowments*: self-awareness, imagination, conscience and independent will. Covey's definition of each is introduced and summarized below; and in addition, I have complemented each with a perspective about Frankl's lived experiences in concentration camps.

Self-awareness

"…the ability to think about your very thought process."[31] We have the ability to stand outside ourselves, to observe the self as a completely different person. This allows us to internalize our thinking. This particular endowment is what enables us to learn from our experiences as well as those from other people.

Viktor Frankl exercised his ability to stand outside himself and discovered, in his own horrific experiences, liberating principles such as the *last of the human freedoms*.

Imagination

"…the ability to create in our minds beyond our present reality."[32] We leverage this endowment to form images and perceptions in our minds. Imagination is the key to understanding and discovering meaning in our experiences.

Frankl utilized imagination as a means to escape the reality of his incarceration, by imagining his wife's image, which he describes "with uncanny acuteness." [33] With the endowment of self-awareness, Frankl discovered "…that love is the ultimate and highest goal to which man can aspire." [34] He leveraged his imagination to find meaning in his suffering and purpose in his life. For example, when almost in tears from physical pain, Frankl projected his thoughts into the future and imagined himself in a warm classroom lecturing about prisoner psychology in concentration camps. This exercise of imagination provided him with a future goal to look forward to and, in turn, he discovered his reason to keep going.

Conscience

"…a deep inner awareness of right and wrong, of the principles that govern our behavior, and a sense of the degree to which our thoughts and actions are in harmony with them."[35] How we respond to life's challenges is influenced by what we perceive is *right* or *wrong*.

107

Frankl refers to conscience as "wisdom of the heart."[36] Conscience helps us to discover meaning, not only in our lives, but in our suffering.

Independent Will

"…the ability to act based on our self-awareness, free of all other influences."[37] That is, human beings have the ability to do what they want to do or what they don't want to do.

Frankl speaks of a particular experience where he reflects on men in the huts who, under terrible conditions, would walk around comforting others, offering up their last piece of bread. This is a powerful depiction of independent will.

ROAD TO HEALING

Covey's proactive model illustrates the *last of the human freedoms*: the power to choose how we respond to life's challenges. When I reflect on my own personal experience in this disorder, I realize that I was *reactive* in my thinking. My behavior was a product of my conditions – influenced by my emotions. At that time, I never truly understood the *last of the human freedoms* principle, but now, I regard it as an essential condition to healing in depression.

The moment I truly accepted responsibility for my own life, I felt empowered. I began to replace *limiting* beliefs with *liberating* beliefs. I focused on how I could leverage Covey's Proactive Model so I, too, could learn to make conscious choices that are "carefully thought about, selected and internalized."[38]

I became proactive in my thinking and responsible in my decision making. This provided me with the necessary confidence to start climbing the ladder within my figurative Deep Well of Depression. With time, I discovered new perspectives that would serve to help me leverage the *last of the human freedoms* principle in my healing journey – perspectives which I applied directly to Covey's Proactive Model.

Expanding on Covey's model, I added to it the following new components: *family and third-party awareness, shock emotion (i.e. emotional intelligence)*, and *motivator factor*. With these new perspectives added, I renamed the expanded model: The Proactive-Liberation Model for Depression.

The Proactive-Liberation Model for Depression

STIMULUS ⟹ FREEDOM TO CHOOSE ⟹ RESPONSE

- Awareness
    - Self
    - Family
    - Third-party
- Shock Emotion
  (Emotional Intelligence)
- Imagination
- Conscience
- Independent Will
    - Motivator Factor

Awareness

I expanded on Covey's proactive model to include a broader range of awareness, in which I've labelled: *self, family* and *third-party awareness*. The awareness endowment can include the act of *extrospection*, that is, putting yourself in somebody else's shoes. This could be in the context of putting yourself in the shoes of a family member or an unrelated individual (third-party member). However, the key behind distinguishing these three levels of awareness is to isolate the relative degrees of emotional investment that you have in each.

For example, you are more emotionally vested in yourself, followed by your family, and are relatively less vested in third-party members that make up your network of friends, colleagues and community. It is not to suggest that your friends don't matter, but in a life or death situation, your family would come first. In this context, we can effectively create three distinct levels of awareness and extract three distinct emotional intensities that can help to produce a greater depth of awareness with respect to how we choose to respond to life's challenges.

In Chapter 9 for example, I describe in intimate detail my defibrillator experience by way of leveraging the human endowment of self-awareness. This enabled me to step outside myself and observe myself as though I was a completely different person. I could envision standing in the basement, staring at myself sitting in the dim-lit corner of the basement, holding my guitar.

While in this state of *introspection*, I could intimately feel *his* pain – *my* pain. Through *self-awareness*, I was able to experience a strong emotional connection. I expanded this endowment of self-awareness to *family* and *third-party awareness*. Through *family awareness*, I was able to put myself in my wife's shoes, so to speak, and take into consideration how my depression was affecting her. By stepping outside myself and observing the bigger picture, I was able to see how difficult things were for her when I was unable to contribute effectively, both as a husband and as a parent. I perceived that my depressive condition was the source of her sorrow and that created sadness in me because of my high emotional investment in her and my children.

By leveraging *third-party awareness,* I was able to observe how my disorder was impacting those outside my family circle – like friends, colleagues and community in general. Though relevant, the level of emotional intensity at this level is lower relative to the emotional investment in self and family.

An illustration of the endowment of self-awareness is that of Ebenezer Scrooge's spiritual journey with the ghosts of Christmas past and present, from Charles Dickens' novel *A Christmas Carol.* In these particular segments, Scrooge is escorted by the spirits and forced to observe his regretful behavior – past and present. By this experience, he was able to see for himself how his behavior was affecting his family and community.

In real life, however, we do not have the luxury of relying on spirits to help us see things for what they truly are. When struggling with depression, we are required to be proactive in our thinking. That is, we must guide ourselves by leveraging the human endowment of self-awareness so we can witness how our behavior is affecting not only ourselves, but those around us. This exercise serves as a precursor to the next component of the expanded Proactive Model: *shock emotion.*

111

Shock Emotion

What I refer to as *shock emotion* is an exercise of *emotional intelligence* (i.e. the ability to control or regulate your emotions in any given circumstance). It is the conscious effort to separate your *thoughts* from your *feelings* in response to an action or stimulus. The conscious ability to separate your emotions from your thought process allows you to contemplate objective, well thought out choices to help you respond to life's challenges more effectively.

This requires you to become proactive in your thinking. I use the term *shock emotion* because emotional intelligence requires that when we feel a disempowering emotion, we must leverage the endowment of self-awareness to separate ourselves from that emotion. From this safe distance, we immediately *shock it* and then contain it. It is an exercise of disallowing your emotion to influence your behavior or determine how you are going to respond. By exercising emotional intelligence, you can spare yourself the anxiety, regret and guilt that sometimes come from acting out on emotion, like losing control of your temper. When you *lose control* and allow your conditions to determine your behavior, this is indicative of low emotional intelligence.

In my struggle with depression, the earliest time in which I consciously shocked an emotion was soon after my defibrillator experience, when I made a commitment to my wife that I would call my doctor for help. I immediately felt the emotion of fear, and I was afraid to pick up the phone. However, through self-awareness, I was able to shock that limiting emotion − fear. I didn't hide from it nor did I pretend it wasn't there; rather, I acknowledged it and respected it in relation to my disorder. I understood why I was feeling that way and made a conscious decision to be proactive in my decision-making by not allowing fear to influence how I was going to respond. Instead, I replaced it with an empowering emotion of *courage* and for the first time in a very, very long time, I felt in control of my disorder.

Imagination

I leveraged the endowment of imagination to replay my defibrillator experience in my mind as if I were watching a movie. Like Scrooge with the Spirit of Christmas Past, I stood there in the basement, observing myself bawling in the corner of that dim-lit room-while my wife comforted me, whispering that it was all going to be alright. Imagination is a valuable tool because it unearths very real emotions associated with a particular experience from the past and, when combined with the endowment of self-awareness, provides the stage for introspection. This allowed me to extract, from my defibrillator experience, both meaning and purpose in my life. In her innocence, my little girl reached out to me and made me realize that my disorder was hurting her and that she needed me back in her life.

Imagination also allowed me to visualize beyond my present reality, to see for myself my purpose in life which I have since discovered is to help liberate others from depressive symptoms. Through the power of imagination, I can see with crystal-clear vision things that haven't even happened yet, such as writing and publishing a book and speaking professionally in front of crowds. Every day I envision myself on stage in front of hundreds of people, helping them in some capacity to improve their lives and take those essential steps toward overcoming symptoms of depression. I see myself speaking of the principles that I had written about in a book – which I envision holding in my hand.

113

When I imagine all of this, it makes me *feel* good. I feel emotions like fulfillment, excitement and joy, as though I had already accomplished these goals.

Another important attribute of this endowment is the ability to contemplate future consequences associated with making what may be perceived are *wrong* choices. Again, in the context of *A Christmas Carol*, this attribute of imagination is utilized when Scrooge is escorted by the Ghost of Christmas Yet to Come, who visualizes his future –a lonesome and condemning fate (in the absence of repentance).

Conscience

Covey states that through self-awareness and conscience, we become *aware* of our weaknesses or areas in our lives that we need to change or do something about. Conscience is about acknowledging that we *should* do what feels *right*. This, of course, is subjective and is determined by one's own values. It should be noted that it is not about *doing* it, but rather acknowledging that we *should* do it. I knew, based on my self-awareness exercise, that calling my doctor was the *right* thing to do, not only for me, but for my family. It does not necessarily mean that I would have to do it, but rather, I knew it was something that I *should* do.

Independent Will

Covey further states that the endowments of *imagination* and *independent will* serve as the vehicles for action, to *act* on our awareness of what needs to be changed in our lives.

The endowments of self-awareness and conscience made me realize that something was not quite right with my thinking, and that I *should* seek help. Through imagination, I was able to envision myself at each stage of the process: picking up the phone and calling the doctor's office, telling my doctor's assistant that I am struggling with depression, booking an appointment, and driving to his office for the appointment. I could imagine the possible questions that he would ask me, which in turn, stimulated fear and anxiety. As a result, I envisioned a very difficult meeting.

Independent will is the trigger for action. It is the trump of all endowments, meaning that although I may recognize that I am struggling with a mental disorder, and realize that seeing my doctor is the *right* thing to do, it is the endowment of *independent will* that bridges the gap between *knowing* and *doing*. Regardless of what I think I should do, I have the ability to act independently of conscience and imagination. In my case, I utilized my independent will, and called my doctor. However, I could have decided just as freely not to call and continue thinking that I would somehow *figure it out*. Independent will is a powerful endowment that grants you the ability to choose to do what you want to do or alternatively, to choose to do what you don't want to do.

Motivator Factor

I have included the factor of motivation as a means to help leverage the endowment of independent will in the decision-making process. The *motivator factor* is a specific and clearly defined goal that you wholeheartedly want to achieve, but which first requires that you make the appropriate, value-driven response (choice) before you can actually realize it.

The anticipated joy from achieving this goal must be greater than the perceived pain (fear) associated with having to make the necessary choice. Following my defibrillator experience, for example, I discovered my *motivator factor: to get better so I can build a snowman with my little girl.* This provided incredible leverage when exercising my independent will, empowering me to make the necessary choices to achieve my goal. This meant picking up the phone and calling my doctor. I had a crystal-clear goal in mind and I knew that unless I was prepared to do what I didn't want to do, that is, unless I was prepared to physically pick up the phone and dial that number, I wouldn't be able to achieve my goal.

LEVERAGING THE PROACTIVE LIBERATION MODEL FOR DEPRESSION

We are now approaching the final stage of my G.E.T. Healthy! approach: "Take Action". We will examine in detail the seven (action) steps that make up the Ladder of Liberation. Each step, or rung, on the ladder requires that we leverage the Proactive-Liberation Model for Depression in order to make "carefully thought about, selected and internalized" choices in our healing process.

The chapters that follow may require you to challenge your own belief system – perhaps requiring you to make choices that you don't want to make. You may feel that you can't follow through on a certain decision out of fear, or some other limiting emotion. However, leveraging the proactive-liberation model enables you to empower your endowments – especially your independent will – when having to make difficult, value-based decisions in your life. Truly understand that you own the freedom to choose – that you are unconditionally *free* to make choices when responding to life's challenges. Remind yourself that you are responsible for your life – recalling Covey's disambiguation of the word responsibility: "…the ability to choose your response."[39]

Remember that you are never alone on this journey. Believe that there is a way out of the Deep Well of Depression should you *choose* to reach for the ladder. Be aware, however, that letting go and plunging back into the Dark Water of Despair should now be perceived as a *conscious choice* – no longer a systematic consequence of depression. Why? Because you are currently aware of something that you may not have recognized before reading this book: *the power to choose* principle. Your endowments of self-awareness and conscience make you aware that you need help; however, it is imagination and independent will that enables you to choose to take action – to fight for liberation from symptoms of depression.

Your success in the final stage of healing begins by leveraging what you should now recognize is the most powerful freedom that every human being possesses: *your freedom to choose.*

CHAPTER 8

Unweaving Depressive Symptoms:
A Perspective

The Ladder of Liberation serves to symbolize a *way out* of the Deep Well of Depression. But what does climbing this figurative ladder really mean in the literal context? I believe it to mean a conscious and proactive approach to *unweaving* the interlocking *strands* of symptoms and emotions that bind together, taking the form of this thing called depression.

My approach to the unweaving process in this context is to develop a system that first alleviates the smothering effect of certain emotions that cultivates depressive symptoms, and then replaces them with empowering emotions to reduce the presence of symptoms. This unweaving system leverages the following three resources: neurovegetative symptoms (from Chapter 2), common emotions associated with symptoms of depression, and the seven rungs on the figurative Ladder of Liberation. These are presented below:

Neurovegetative symptoms

- Sleep disorder (either increased or decreased sleep)
- Interest deficit (anhedonia)
- Guilt (worthlessness, hopelessness, regret)
- Energy deficit
- Concentration deficit
- Appetite disorder (either decreased or increased)
- Psychomotor retardation or agitation
- Suicidality

Symptoms and emotions associated with depression
(Note: accompanying definitions derived from Merriam-Webster Dictionary[8])

Agitation - a state of excessive psychomotor activity accompanied by increased tension and irritability

Regret - to be very sorry for (something you've done, said or caused to happen)

Irritability - quick excitability to annoyance, impatience, or anger

Fatigue - weariness or exhaustion from labor, exertion, or stress

119

Guilt - a feeling of culpability (meaning: meriting condemnation or blame especially as wrong or harmful) for offenses

Hopelessness - having no expectation of good or success

Worthlessness - lacking moral or personal value

Restlessness - characterized by or manifesting unrest especially of mind

Fear - an unpleasant often strong emotion caused by anticipation or awareness of danger

Suicidality - marked by an impulse to commit suicide (meaning: the act or an instance of taking one's own life voluntarily and intentionally)

Dejection - lowness of spirits

Sadness - affected with or expressive of grief or unhappiness

Disappoint - to fail to meet the expectation or hope (of someone)

Despair - to lose all hope or confidence

Resentment - a feeling of indignant displeasure or persistent ill will at something regarded as a wrong, insult, or injury

Shame - a painful emotion caused by consciousness of guilt, shortcoming, or impropriety

Seven rungs on the *Ladder of Liberation*

Step 1: Defibrillate your depression

Step 2: Get help

Step 3: Forgive yourself

Step 4: Create a goal to look forward to

Step 5: Leverage exercise to alleviate depressive symptoms

Step 6: Embrace the good in your life

Step 7: Give back and help others

Conceptually, each of these symptoms of depression and enduring emotions serves as a single strand that, when tightly woven together, forms this disorder called depression.

THE LOGIC BEHIND 'UNWEAVING' SYMPTOMS

It stands to reason that the more strands of enduring emotions that I can learn to unweave in this disorder, the more I can reshape and influence its debilitating effects. To illustrate this idea, recall the Depression Severity Range Scale model introduced in chapter 2:

Depression Severity Range Scale

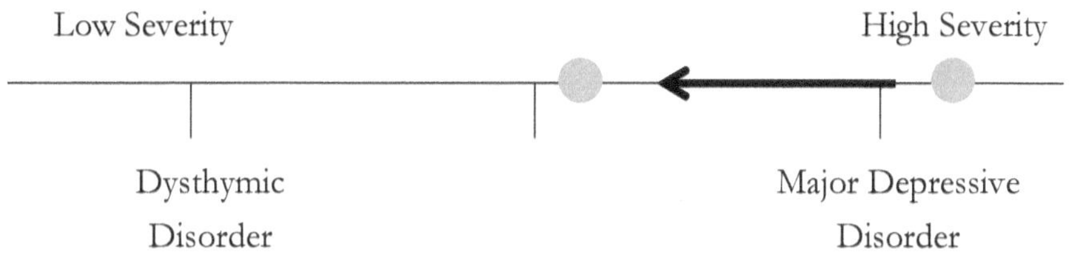

If through this system we can learn to successfully unweave certain debilitating emotions and symptoms, like guilt, suicidality, and interest deficit for example, the more I believe we can influence its severity. In other words, we can use this unweaving process to reshape depression by unweaving the countless strands of underlying and persistent emotions, thereby influencing the level of severity on the Depression Severity Range Scale. Conceptually, this means we can influence the position of the dot – toward a lower point of severity, as illustrated.

Every step we take on the Ladder of Liberation effectively disrupts the consistent pattern of negative thinking – which otherwise serves to sustain depressive symptoms. This disruption enables us to replace limiting beliefs with empowering beliefs, and this in turn influences healthy thinking patterns and produces positive emotions.

Theoretically, the first rung on the Ladder of Liberation is *Defibrillate your depression* which would serve to unweave the associated symptom of *worthlessness*, replacing it with a contradicting, but empowering, affirmation of *self-worth*. The second rung, *Get help*, serves to unweave emotions like *fear* and *shame*, replacing them instead with *courage* and *dignity*. The third rung is *Forgive yourself*, to unweave the enduring emotion of *guilt*, replacing it with *empathy*. The fourth rung is *Create a goal to look forward to*, which replaces *hopelessness* with the empowering affirmation of *hope*. And so on.

The ultimate goal in this exercise is to unweave as many strands of enduring emotions and symptoms as possible; and replace them with empowering emotions produced by a proactive and responsible belief system. By this exercise, I believe we reduce depression severity by disabling its underlying symptoms and persistent emotions.

THE UNWEAVING PROCESS IN PRACTICE

My defibrillator experience (described next in Chapter 9) produced a powerful unweaving effect in my disorder. My belief that my family was better off without me produced the neurovegetative symptom of *worthlessness*. However, when my daughter reached out to me, I was immediately overcome by an emotional disturbance stemming from the implied contradiction to this belief. That is, she made me believe instead that my family was better off <u>with</u> me. This produced a wave of contradicting and empowering emotions from my newly-adopted belief that I am *valued* or of *worth* in my life. My defibrillator experience enabled me to not only unweave, or disempower, a debilitating depressive symptom, but it enabled me to *trump* it with an incredibly powerful belief.

Before I made the proactive choice to pick up the phone and seek help for my condition, I *felt* the emotion of fear. This fear was formed by my belief that depression was something to be embarrassed about, and in my reactive mindset, it prevented me from wanting to pick up the phone. But by leveraging the Proactive-Liberation Model for Depression, I was able to make an informed, value-based decision – one that served to overshadow my initial feeling of fear. This enabled me to leverage the endowment of *independent will* to override my fear and pick up the phone. I was able to replace a limiting and persistent feeling with an empowering emotion like *courage* – produced from a proactive and responsible belief that I don't have to feel embarrassed about my disorder.

STAGE 3

TAKE ACTION

CHAPTER 9

Action Step #1: 'Defibrillate' your Depression

In the Deep Well of Depression, your defibrillator moment is triggered by *something* that sends shockwaves through your heart with an impact so powerful that it forces you to pull your head out of the water in a whiplash motion. It is in this powerful moment that you can release the Weeds of Damaging Beliefs from your grip, lift your head out of the Dark Water of Despair, and consciously reach for the Rope of Support with all of your strength.

Your defibrillator experience is your *wake-up call* and represents the very first action step toward achieving liberation from depressive symptoms. I believe that the underlying purpose is to instill, temporarily, a surge of *hope* in an otherwise hopeless mindset.

REACHING OUT: THE NOT SO SIMPLE TASK

For the person treading the Dark Water of Despair in the Deep Well of Depression, the seemingly simple task of reaching for the rope is not so simple. As one may appreciate, this can be a considerable cause of frustration for his supporters holding onto the Rope of Support because they cannot understand why this person won't simply just hold on to the rope so they can pull him out of the well. Part of the frustration stems from a lack of understanding, not only about the complexity of this disorder, but about one dangerous and disabling threat that can occur: *identify transformation.*

The Threat of "Identity Transformation"

For a person struggling with depression, his supporters may not realize that the longer he treads the Dark Water of Despair, or in literal terms, the longer his symptoms go unresolved, the greater the threat this disorder will alter his true identity. In his book *Awaken the Giant Within,* Anthony Robbins explains this potentially dangerous threat:

"Many people stop fighting their painful emotions and decide to fully indulge in them...It becomes a 'badge of courage'...It literally becomes part of their identity, a way of being unique; they begin to pride themselves on being worse off than anyone else...this is one of the deadliest traps of all...it becomes a self-fulfilling prophecy where the person ends up having an investment in feeling bad on a regular basis…they are truly trapped."[40]

In my experience with depression, one factor preventing me from reaching for the Rope of Support was because feeling bad all the time evolved into an empowering psychological investment. Why? Because my master was effective in his efforts to convince me not to care about anything or anyone, because – as my master would relentlessly affirm – no one cared about me.

When exposed to such painful assertions, especially for a prolonged period of time, your cognitive defenses can't help but weaken, and you begin to question your significance in life. Eventually, it hardens you. And in a strange turn of events, you begin to extract from this 'defeatism attitude' a dark sense of empowerment. The danger in this state of thinking, however, was how I regarded my life with such indifference. My attitude while sporting this *badge of courage*, or alternatively, my *badge of depression*, was infected. In one sense, it felt empowering because I discovered my excuse for giving up or blaming others and my conditions. Ironically, this provided me with some sense of comfort in my misery.

When I first read that passage from Anthony Robbins, I felt as though he saw right through my disguise – exposing me for something that I was not. His passage revealed to me that whatever I was becoming was not who I truly was. It made me realize that the longer I stood behind my badge of depression, the closer I got to losing out in my life. I woke to the realization that I was, indeed, truly trapped in my disorder. At least this was the case up until I experienced my defibrillator moment in

127

depression – the night my daughter reached out to me and shattered my badge of depression into a thousand tiny pieces.

HOW TO 'DEFIBRILLATE' YOUR DEPRESSION

In my personal battle with depression, there was no single rung on that Ladder of Liberation that produced anything like the mushroom cloud of emotion that erupted inside of me the night I experienced my defibrillator moment. Those simple, innocent words from my daughter detonated in me a shockwave so powerful that it completely demolished the very walls that stood to defend this self-destructive identity that I confided in.

In hindsight, I've come to realize how fortunate I was because my defibrillator experience seemingly happened *for* me - at least, this is what I had initially thought. Indeed, no combination of words could come anywhere close to explaining the impact it had on me while incapacitated in my deep, dark well. But now, I'm not so convinced that it just happened *for* me. Rather, I believe it just *happened* because my mindset was in the right place at the right time in that right moment.

What I mean is, at that moment while standing on the deck with my little girl, my head was temporarily raised from the Dark Water of Despair just long enough to consciously hear and process her words – and *feel* the underlying meaning of those words. This *feeling* is represented by the tiny beam of sunlight that stretches down from the opening of the well. At this depth, it radiates only the slightest degree of the sun's warmth. But it was just enough to *feel* it *momentarily*. I believe that this feeling is what detonated my defibrillator experience. Had I not, in that moment, appreciated the presence of my little girl's company, my head may have remained submerged and I might possibly have missed what turned out to be the most important experience of my life.

I certainly appreciate that defibrillator experiences such as mine may not happen to others in the same fashion. However, I do believe that they do happen, and sometimes, we miss the signs because we are not focused on that tiny beam of light when the right time presents itself. So to truly achieve a defibrillator experience, I believe it first requires you to lift your head from the Dark Water of Despair; and second, that you focus on the tiny beam of sunlight.

Lift Your Head

I begin this section with a question: *What are you willing to give up in your life that makes holding on to your 'badge of depression' worth it?*

You have to give up something because every facet of your life is affected by depression. This *badge* can enable you to feed off of the sincere worries and concerns that your family and friends feel for you. How do I know this? Because I was in that place – fully indulging in my symptoms and painful emotions. But the one thing I didn't acknowledge was how I was truly affecting those around me – the *depth* in which I was affecting the people in my life that truly cared for me.

For example, my wife told me during a low point in my disorder that she felt tremendous guilt for how I was hurting. At the time, I couldn't effectively communicate my pain which made it even more difficult for her – trying to figure out for the both of us why I was so unhappy in my life. In addition to these emotional strains, she had to assume head of household duties during those times when my condition inhibited me

129

from being the father and husband my family needed me to be. I didn't realize until after having experienced my defibrillator moment how my disorder was affecting my children and their behavior. While incapacitated in my dark place, I wasn't able to be there for my family. I just wasn't there.

There came a point in my disorder where I had to decide whether I was prepared to sacrifice my relationship with my family in order to stay submerged in the Dark Water of Despair. I had to contemplate some difficult questions: *Are you prepared to turn your back on your little girl and your family just so you can have an excuse to give up on your life?* My heart (that is, my conscience) had an answer: *You have no right to give up on anything or anyone! And you especially have no right to give up on yourself! Why? Because you will deprive the very people in your life that you love of the true value and worth that lies within you! You just need to open your eyes and see it for yourself!*

While treading water in the Deep Well of Depression, you have no concept of how important you truly are to those around you. Depression, as we well know, is a catalyst for hopelessness, and when you feel hopeless in this disorder, you lack any expectation of good or success in your life. However, you are the only one deceived by this – I was the only person deceived by this. Your supporters, the people holding on to your rope, can *see* your sun so much clearer than you and can *feel* the heat that radiates from it – all that is wonderful in your life.

I believe that before you can genuinely stir up your emotions with such intensity that your own molecular structure becomes so unstable that it ignites an explosive defibrillator experience, you must leverage your inner strength to lift your head, open your eyes and intently focus on that tiny beam of sunlight that occupies your dark space.

In the literal context, this means reaching out to your supporters and talking to them. As difficult as this may very well be, it is important to leverage your human endowments and find the strength to do this. I promise you that your supporters will be so relieved that you reached out to them, and they will be eager to help you in any way they can. Open yourself up and ask some emotionally-driven questions, such as:

Of your spouse or partner: *Why do you still love me? Why are you helping me? What do you see in me? How do you feel right now, about me? How has the way I've been feeling affected you? What do you think about when you see me this way?*

Of you children or dependents: *Are you aware that something is bothering me? How do you feel right now? How do you feel when I look sad? How do you feel when I tell you that I can't play with you because I am too tired or not feeling well?*

Of your friends: *Have you noticed anything different about me lately? How do you feel about it? I'm going through a rough time right now and want to ask: what value do you see in our relationship? What value do you see in me?*

This real-life exercise is represented by you consciously focusing on the tiny beam of sunlight in your dark place. Remain focused on the task at hand, and listen intently to their answers. Truly listen and consciously process the emotion in their responses, the meaning behind their message. This emotional exercise is a condition for the next step: *trigger* your defibrillator experience.

TRIGGER YOUR DEFIBRILLATOR EXPERIENCE

I believe that to trigger your defibrillator moment, you must recognize and embrace a powerfully emotional belief about yourself and your conditions. *When you get better, can you build a snowman with me?* My therapist explained that when my daughter asked me this, she sensed that I was hurting and growing distant in our relationship. So what did she do? She reached out to me. She wanted me closer. She wanted to spend time with her daddy because she loves him and finds comfort in him. And when he is not there for her, she feels hurt.

I was convinced in my sickness that my family would be better off without me, and this very belief generated in me the depressive symptom of *worthlessness*. When my daughter reached out to me, her underlying message that *I want to spend time with you, I miss you and I value you* generated conflicting emotions, like feeling *valued* and of *worth*. As a result, this generated a new and empowering belief that *my family would be better off with me*.

It was this clash within my belief system that triggered my defibrillator experience. This conflict in emotion motivated me to exercise my *independent will* endowment and reach for the Rope of Support.

I believe this to be a critical step in the healing process because it generates a temporary surge of *hope* which, in turn, clashes powerfully with an otherwise *hopeless* mindset. In other words, it provides a window of opportunity – an immediate, but temporary reprieve from oppression in this disorder – enabling you to escape the Dark Water of Despair. By this action, you reach for the Rope of Support and enable your supporters to pull you up to the first rung on the ladder. Suspended, you look down, observing the Piranhas of Depression bashing about, seemingly frustrated by your departure.

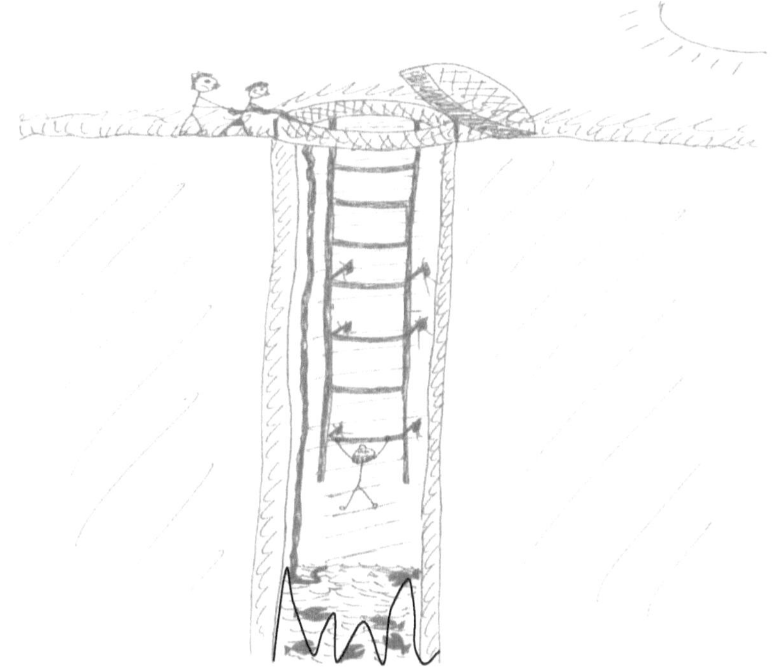

However, when you look up from this vantage point, you can observe the brightness of the Sun that surrounds the opening of the well. This image symbolizes *hope*, that one day you will find yourself on top of the well, exposed to the Sun's radiating warmth – symbolizing true appreciation for all the blessings in your life. You can see the dark outlines of your supporters standing at the surface, encouraging you to pull yourself up to the second rung on the ladder.

Your hands are wet and arms weak from treading water for so long, making it increasingly difficult to hold on to the first ladder rung. Your Rope of Support dangles freely beside you, within reach, should you feel like you're losing grip on the ladder. There are two observations to make after having experienced your defibrillator moment.

Firstly, you have not escaped your perceived challenges or problems. The Piranhas of Depression are still very much alive and remain as aggressive as when you were in the water with them. But now, you see your life's challenges from a different angle or perspective. You now have a "bird's eye view" of the Piranhas of Depression as you hang freely from the first rung on the ladder. This is a stark contrast to when you were in the water with them anxiously awaiting each successive bite. The point being, by hanging from the ladder, you are in a relatively better position.

The second observation to make is that you remain vulnerable to letting go. As you hang freely from this first rung, your hands and arms are tired from treading water while maintaining your grip on the Weeds of Damaging Beliefs. What this means is that you are vulnerable to falling because you have nothing to *stand on* – that is, there is no rung below you on which you can support your feet.

Your defibrillator moment provided you with a sense of *hope* in your disorder by challenging the way you think. But unless you are willing to take action - that is, unless you are ready to apply what you have learned about the *last of the human freedoms* and *choose* to start climbing the Ladder of Liberation, then it is just a matter of time before your grip loosens and you let go, plunging back into the Dark Water of Despair. But be warned: *letting go*, you must now realize, is an exercise of the most powerful endowment you own: independent will. Letting go is now a matter of choice and no longer a systematic consequence of depression. Furthermore, you must understand that letting go now will irritate and invoke a more aggressive behavior from the *Mental/educational* piranha of depression. Why? Because after having gained knowledge in this disorder, now you know better.

No matter what you are going through in your life, whatever it is that has set off the violent attacks by your Piranhas of Depression, you are personally responsible for how you *choose* to respond to your challenges. You are fully responsible for not only the choices you have made, but how you will respond to the resulting consequences. Personally speaking, this was very difficult for me to accept. But I learned in healing that acceptance was essential because, until I stopped blaming others for my perceived problems, and took responsibility for my own life, I was destined to remain hopeless in my disorder.

PUT EVERYTHING INTO YOUR FIRST STEP

It is imperative at this stage in your healing process to begin to take action as soon as possible and begin to pull yourself up to the second rung on the ladder. When you do this, you will have your feet planted securely on the first rung, and from this point on, your chances for success improve tremendously. Planting your feet is symbolic of building confidence and instilling hope in your disorder.

If my healing process is any indication for what you will go through, the climb up the Ladder of Liberation is going to be a very difficult endeavor. However, your confidence will only grow and strengthen with each successive step you make. I assure you that if you are truly prepared to pay the price for freedom in this disorder, your journey in healing will be an amazing and liberating experience that can forever change your life... if you choose to allow it.

135

CHAPTER 10

Action Step #2: Seek Help

I have learned from my experience with depression that the very first physical step toward healing in depression is to *seek help*. This will sound obvious for those who have never treaded water in the Deep Well of Depression, but for a person who suffers in this disorder, it can be a very difficult thing to do.

Depression is a condition that carries with it a perceived stigma which can serve to deter a person from seeking professional help. Prior to experiencing my defibrillator moment, I kept telling myself that I would *figure it out* and that I didn't need to see a *shrink*. I was too proud to admit that I had a problem I couldn't control – believing that lying on a couch talking to a psychiatrist was admission of defeat.

I discovered in hindsight that by adopting this belief, I was only deceiving myself. When I peeled back the layers of ignorance relating to my perception about this disorder, I realized that I was harboring reactive emotions like fear and embarrassment, and allowed them to influence my decision making. I was afraid and ashamed of my condition. I believed that if people were to learn about my depression, they would look at me differently, or look down on me for my perceived *weakness*. I was afraid to be stereotyped.

After my defibrillator experience, I came to the realization that I had a great deal to lose if I allowed my conditions to determine how I was going to respond with respect to my disorder. If things didn't improve, I knew that it would just be a matter of time before I gave up on my family, my career, and possibly my life. I had everything to lose and for what? Because I felt embarrassed? Because I worried about what other people might think about me? I realized that the potential costs greatly outweighed the *perceived* stigma with respect to my depression. I knew that it was time to take control. I had to *choose* to be strong in my disorder and be proactive in my thinking.

The following section outlines what I believe is the necessary framework to transition from a *reactive* thought process to one that is *proactive*.

137

TAKING RESPONSIBILITY

At this stage in the Deep Well of Depression context, after having experienced your defibrillator moment, you are hanging from the first rung on the Ladder of Liberation. Up to this point, you have relied on your supporters to pull you up. Now, you are in a position of responsibility. Recall Covey's disambiguation of that word: "...response-ability – the ability to choose your response."[41] You must now exercise your ability to respond to your disorder by pulling yourself up to the second rung on the Ladder of Liberation. Your leverage – or strength – in this feat is characterized by the conscious act of being *responsible*.

Proactive Belief: "I Am Able To Choose My Response"

By adopting this belief, you instantaneously transition from reactive thinking to a *proactive* state of mind – and recognize a sense of urgency to take effective action with respect to your disorder. When you consciously adopt this proactive belief, you will have successfully unwoven a single, but powerful depressive strand called *hopelessness*, replacing it instead with an empowering strand of *hope*.

This unweaving affect can immediately alter the shape of your depression by strengthening your defenses while simultaneously weakening its effects. In this moment, we begin to pull ourselves up to the second rung – or take that next action step and *seek help*. We do this by leveraging the *Proactive-Liberation Model for Depression*.

Proactive-Liberation Model for Depression: *Seek Help*

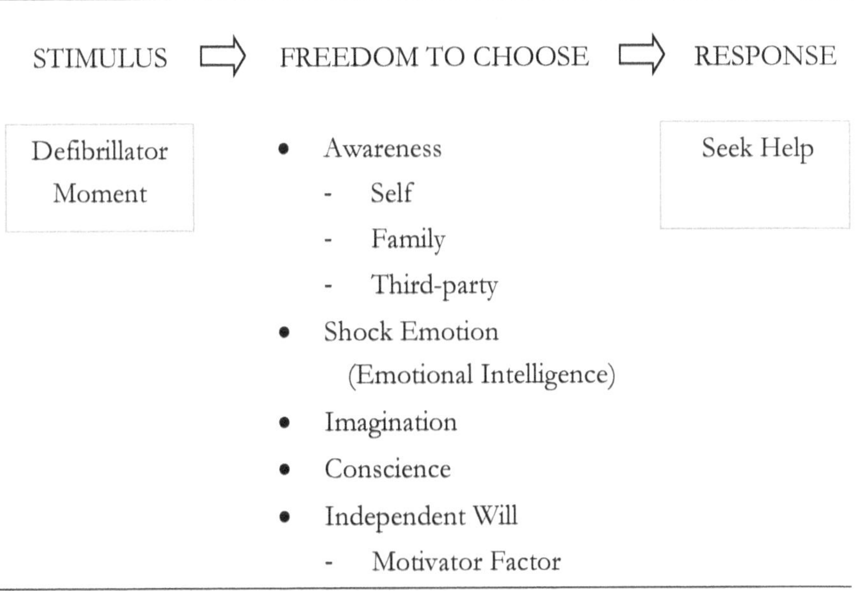

Our goal at this point is to make a carefully thought about, selected and internalized choice that produces a favorable response, which in this case, is to *physically* seek professional help. We will do this by leveraging our human endowments in the Proactive-Liberation Model for Depression: first by creating awareness about how our condition is affecting us (and those around us); and second, by making a choice and acting on it.

I have a suggestion for you: get a piece of paper (or a journal) and label the page "Step 2: Seek help." Each endowment in the proactive-liberation model for depression will serve as a heading for you to make notes under. This exercise will help you to not only organize your thoughts, but will be an effective medium for communicating (and containing) your feelings and perspectives.

FREEDOM TO CHOOSE ENDOWMENTS

Create Awareness

Self-awareness: We begin this process by taking a few deep breaths. Now envision yourself sitting wherever you are and then proceed to step outside of your person so that you can observe *the other you* from a distance – as if you are standing next to your seated self, like a completely different person. Now summon what I will call the *Spirit of Depression Past*, so to speak, and allow the spirit to *show* you certain experiences of what this third-person version of *you* has been going through with respect to their depression.

With respect to my own experience, this would be like the spirit placing me in a specific memory of my disorder so I could observe *my* behavior during this particularly difficult time. For example, the spirit would escort me to a time when the *other me* was crying in the car on the way to work. I can observe this as though I am sitting next to *him* in the passenger seat (and the spirit sitting in the back!). He can't see me, but I can see and *feel* him. In this introspective exercise, it makes me feel sad watching him like this – wishing I could somehow talk to him and tell him everything is going to be okay. But in *his* time dimension, I can't. I can only watch, helplessly.

What experiences do you encounter when the spirit escorts you through the painful terrain of your depression? Describe in intimate detail what you feel in these experiences – or how you perceive the *other you* is feeling while captivated in these particularly difficult frames in time.

Allow the spirit of depression past to guide your pen so you can filter whatever it is that you are thinking and feeling with respect to your disorder and your conditions. I believe this to be an incredibly powerful exercise because writing enables you to express painful emotions and divert them away from yourself and onto paper. I explained in chapter four that I conditioned myself from an early age to suppress difficult emotions, filtering them inward and toward myself. This was a very unhealthy approach to coping with life's challenges which ultimately deteriorated my mental health over time. Writing, however, allowed me to communicate these feelings and express myself in ways in which my disorder inhibited. Writing served as a loophole in my disorder, so to speak. I wrote everything down – my thoughts, perspectives and about my depression and how it was affecting not only my life, but others'. In a strange sort of way, this exercise served as a medium of communication and understanding between two beings of the same person: the conscious me and the *other me* who occupies my most difficult memories.

The most important thing with respect to this exercise is to be honest and true when writing about your feelings and perspectives this way. The idea is to write to yourself as though you are explaining your thoughts to a completely different person – trying to make them aware of how your disorder has affected you and offering insight as to what goes through your mind when reflecting on your experiences.

141

Family awareness: The next step in this exercise is putting yourself in someone else's shoes with respect to your depression – specifically, your family's shoes. You are now encouraged to document in writing how you *think* your condition is affecting those you love.

This exercise requires you to switch places with a loved one and evaluate in intimate detail how you would feel if it was your spouse or child experiencing the same depressive symptoms that you are struggling with. Write out how it would make you feel knowing that your spouse was feeling hopeless in her life, or if you had a child exhibiting suicidal thoughts. How would this make you feel? What emotions would you generate from this deeply disturbing exercise? Anxiety? Concern? Helplessness? Sadness? It is important to be honest in your description because the underlying purpose of this profoundly emotional and difficult exercise is to make you aware of how your suffering is affecting those who love you as deeply as you love them. This is important because unless you learn to reach out, your loved ones will have no idea what is happening to you, or the extent to which you are suffering. The *not knowing* can generate feelings of helplessness and produce *worst case scenario* thinking patterns, further compounding their concern and worry about your health and safety.

Continuing with the *family awareness* exercise, imagine a family member who is suffering with alcohol addiction and ask yourself the following question: what could your loved one do for themselves that would relieve the concerning emotions you would have for them as a result of their condition? Perhaps seek help? Wouldn't you feel considerable joy learning that they made a proactive choice to attend an *Alcoholics Anonymous* meeting? Now reverse the role: if you were that person suffering with alcoholism, would you now have a clearer perception about what you *should* do to help spare your loved ones further worry and anxiety, and afford them the same joyful experience knowing that you are taking action steps to get better? Now write down what you feel you could do to help ease the troubling emotions your family is feeling for you as a result of your depression.

Third-party awareness: In this reflection exercise, now it is time to put yourself in the shoes of those outside your family unit. These could include co-workers, friends, social groups and so on. Possible questions to consider:

How would you feel if a friend was suffering with depression and interacted with you the way you have been interacting with her? How would it make you feel to learn she was afraid to talk to you about it out of fear you might feel differently about her?

Describe in detail how you would feel in this situation knowing that a friend was experiencing terrible anguish and that she was afraid to reach out to you for help.

Conscience: By exercising the endowment of awareness in this Proactive-Liberation Model for Depression, you should be able to recognize in your heart what the *right* thing to do is with respect to healing in your disorder. Conscience is your heart telling you what it is you need to do in order to make things better - not just for your sake, but for your family's sake as well. At this time, be honest and write down what your heart is telling you. The question is simple: What *should* you do? The answer may not be so simple to admit, but write down plausible options. Remember at this stage, you do not have to act on anything – you just need to be aware at this point of how your disorder is affecting you, your family, and your community, and recognize what it is you *should* do to improve your condition.

Now it is time to contemplate *action* in this exercise. The next stage is to leverage the proactive-liberation model to determine *how* to take the necessary action that you are consciously aware you need to take.

Take Action

Imagination: We will now leverage our endowment of imagination, which Covey explains, is "…the ability to create in our minds beyond our present reality."[42] In our present state, we imagine vividly each perceived step that we must take in order to achieve our goal, which is to position our feet securely on the Ladder of Liberation by the act of *seeking help*. In my own experience, I imagined myself picking up the phone and talking to my doctor's assistant; booking an appointment; arriving at the medical center; and finally, sitting down to talk with my doctor about my depression. This was the roadmap I had envisioned using my imagination – a pathway guided by my *conscious self*. I was indeed fearful about the things I didn't know or expect, like what I would say to my doctor, but that didn't matter in the moment: I just needed to see a clear path to my desired destination.

At this time, leverage your own imagination and map out the steps that you will need to take to satisfy the *seek help* condition of your journey. Focus less on the roadblocks, and more on creating, in your present reality, your pathway to fulfilling the goal of seeking medical support.

I believe it is equally important to use our imagination to create a deep emotional disturbance by envisioning, in our present reality, the very real consequences should we ignore our conscience and choose <u>not</u> to seek help. What are the possible real risks for being reactive in your depression? Imagine yourself letting go from the Ladder of Liberation and falling back into the Dark Water of Despair. How long before the relentless attacks by your Piranhas of Depression break you down – worse than ever before?

Use your imagination and write down some very real consequences of doing nothing. What do you stand to lose in your life by surrendering to your *master* in depression? If you were to resort to alcohol or drugs to help cope with your *piranhas,* for example, what would be some possible consequences? Think about your family walking out on you because of your troubled behavior. Extend your imagination further and envision your kids growing bitter towards you and the life path you *chose* – and unforgiving because you weren't there for them when they needed you the most. Dare to vividly imagine the most disturbing image of all: the sensation of the barrel of a gun pressed against your temple seconds before you make that last-ditch effort to escape the relentless attacks by your Piranhas of Depression. Unsettling, isn't it? Sometimes we need to resort to an uncomfortable depth of disturbance in order to find the resolve to put into action what your conscious is guiding you to do. Imagination is a powerful tool we can leverage to empower or disturb.

Shock emotion: When I vividly imagined myself picking up the phone to call my doctor's office, I was overcome with fear. In this moment, aided by my emotional disturbance (such as that described in the preceding section), I recognized that this was the time that I needed to be proactive in my thinking and exercise *emotional intelligence* – which, to

145

put it simply, is the conscious ability to manage emotions in order to make *value-based* decisions when responding to life's challenges. This is in contrast to making emotionally-driven choices which I might later regret.

I immediately *shocked* and destabilized my fear, and the endowment of self-awareness enabled me to step back, and acknowledge why I was feeling fearful in the first place. By internalizing my thinking in this way, I recognized clearly what the right choice was, and then made it happen by being proactive and responsible.

Independent will: Covey describes that a person's *will to choose* exists independently of all other endowments. Simply speaking, you are free to make a value-based decision and call your doctor, and you are equally free to make an emotionally-based decision and <u>not</u> call, perhaps out of fear. Remember that with conscience, you are aware of what the *right* thing is to do; however, it is not, in and of itself, a deciding factor.

I can speak from personal experience that it can be incredibly difficult to pick up the phone and make that call. A person who has never struggled with depression cannot fully appreciate the emotional strain that ensues when, after dialing, you're required to give the reason for the appointment. One cannot understand the vulnerability you feel, echoing in the tone of your voice, as you try to respond without breaking down. And one cannot fully appreciate the liberating tears that follow once the reality sets in that you *did it!*

Motivator factor: I believe that it is essential in healing to clearly define a goal that speaks very deeply to your heart. In Chapter 7, I described the concept of a motivator factor: a specific and clearly defined goal that you wholeheartedly want to achieve, but requires you to make the appropriate, value-driven choices before actually realizing it.

Your *motivator factor* must be something that you have an enormous emotional investment in. My little girl's words: *when you get better, can you build a snowman with me?* served as my *motivator factor* when I needed to dig deep and make some very difficult decisions along my journey. It provided me with a future goal to look forward to: *to get better so I can build a snowman with my little girl.* This in turn equipped me with incredible strength and courage to keep climbing the ladder in my Deep Well of Depression – even during those times when I felt like letting go. My *motivator factor* was what anchored my grip on each rung on the ladder – and what motivated me to keep climbing.

Ladder of Liberation Step 2: Action Steps to Seek Help

1. *Talk about it*

If you haven't already done so, approach someone you trust (e.g. family member, friend, colleague, priest, etc.) and request a time when you can be alone to talk about something that is important to you. This will establish a supporter in your Deep Well of Depression - someone that will hold the Rope of Support for you as you climb the Ladder of Liberation.

2. *Be proactive in mind*

Be consciously aware that you have the freedom to choose your response under any circumstance. If you choose to follow and use the Proactive-Liberation Model for Depression, I believe that you will be better positioned to make value-based choices during those difficult times in your disorder.

3. *Talk to your doctor*

This is a crucial step in your healing. Your supporter will be there to listen to you and provide you with a shoulder to cry on, but you cannot expect them to treat a serious condition such as this. I have learned in my own personal experience that the severity of depression can worsen if left untreated. It is important to act on this disorder immediately. Be proactive: call your doctor's office and secure that appointment.

4. *Prepare to open up*

It is absolutely essential to be as honest as possible to your doctor when posed with some very difficult questions. Before your doctor can refer you to psychiatric counseling, they must first ask a series of diagnostic questions to help them determine the severity of your condition. This, I remember from my experience, was the single most difficult step in my healing process.

I vividly remember being in the examination room, sitting across from my doctor, and struggling to communicate daunting answers to some very tough questions. I had to reach deep to find the strength to trench through the emotional turmoil I was experiencing - the tears, the shaking, and uncontrolled twitching. As I described in an earlier chapter, upon finishing my appointment, I met my wife in the hallway and reached for my three-month old son before crying into his little shoulder. This step was one of the most difficult, yet liberating, experiences I have encountered throughout my climb on the Ladder of Liberation.

CHAPTER 11

Action Step #3: Forgive Yourself

The feeling of guilt (which encompasses emotions of worthlessness, hopelessness, and regret) is identified as a single neurovegetative symptom of major depression and served as one of the most debilitating emotions that I had to contend with in my personal struggle. When you tread water in the Deep Well of Depression, you have gripped tightly in hand Weeds of Damaging Beliefs. And emitting from these weeds are enduring emotions like guilt and regret.

I blamed myself for all the hardships that I experienced throughout my life and as a consequence, I cultivated a deep sense of worthlessness over time. I deeply regretted many life choices that I had made and felt heavily burdened by guilt. I felt like I was failing in just about every aspect of my life – and I especially felt like I was failing my family. Seemingly trapped in this defeatist state of thinking, I was vulnerable. It was not difficult for my master to convince me that *my family would be better off without me.*

We all make mistakes! This is one of those enduring proclamations serving to provide a superficial sense of comfort whenever a perceived *mistake* is committed. Merriam-Webster dictionary defines the word *mistake* as: "to blunder in the choice of."

Thinking in the context of the Proactive-Liberation Model for Depression, a mistake would be committed when choosing to respond to a particular action or stimulus in a way that produces an undesirable consequence. In such an experience, we may generate a belief that *I was wrong to react that way* which in turn, may produce undesirable emotions of guilt and regret. Depending on the perceived severity of the consequence, a mistake can haunt a person their entire lives and can serve to greatly alter or influence not only how we think about ourselves, but how we think we are perceived by others.

THE GUILTY CONSCIENCE: "GHOST OF GUILT" PARADIGM

We have learned that conscience is an important human endowment that we take into consideration when determining how to respond to a certain action or stimulus. It is shaped by our underlying values, or our moral code, if you will, which instinctively points us in what we perceive

151

is the *right* direction. Recall that conscience is an endowment of *awareness*, and not *action*.

Independent will and imagination are endowments of action, and are responsible for putting the *freedom to choose* principle in motion to generate a *response*. When we exercise our will independently of all other endowments, and choose instead to respond contrary to what our conscience is telling us, the consequence is typically a *guilty conscience*. When you realize the consequence of a regretful action or choice, you generate a belief that you made a "terrible mistake," and depending on the severity of the consequence, this can produce some very painful emotions.

I like to think of guilt as a merciless ghost that serves to haunt our thoughts and torments us by consistently flaunting *mistakes* we have made in the past. This Ghost of Guilt is summoned by a guilty conscience, and depending on the severity of the consequence, its presence can be incredibly frightening and incapacitating – emotionally, spiritually and physically.

The Ghost of Guilt serves to make one feel *less of a person* by manipulating one's belief system when most vulnerable to attack. It follows, then, that unless we strive to be proactive and learn to reconcile with this ghost, we risk being at the mercy of its domineering presence.

PROACTIVE RECONCILIATION CONCEPT TO UNWEAVE GUILT

So how do we learn to truly forgive ourselves when we reflect on an experience in our past that generates a seemingly unbreakable belief like *I will never forgive myself for that!?* From my own personal perspective, the neurovegetative symptom of guilt can be one of the most difficult emotional strands to unweave when leveraging the Proactive-Liberation Model for Depression. But I believe that it has to be unwoven, and also replaced with emotions that serve, by contradiction, to empower: like acceptance and forgiveness. Forgiving self is the third step on the Ladder of Liberation and this requires considerable effort in leveraging a proactive thought process.

Before we can attempt to unweave the painful and potentially disabling emotion called guilt, we have to first challenge and displace the very system of limiting beliefs upon which guilt thrives. I believe we can accomplish this by adopting and applying a foundation of proactive, responsible and unwavering beliefs, such as those tabled on the next page, which I've named: Proactive Reconciliation Beliefs (PRBs).

Reactive Beliefs that Empower "Guilt"	Proactive Reconciliation Beliefs that Disempower "Guilt"
I will never forgive myself.	*I am fully responsible for my actions.*
I am a terrible person.	*I will accept the consequences.*
Everyone is going to hate me.	*I will become better because of it.*
I hate myself for this.	*I will 'pay it forward' (help others).*

The proactive reconciliation process for unweaving guilt first begins by recognizing the *chain reaction* that occurs in the Proactive-Liberation Model for Depression – following the onset of an undesirable *consequence*. That is, when we believe we made a "terrible mistake" in how we responded to a particular stimulus, a chain reaction occurs: the *consequence* born from the perceived mistake immediately transforms and becomes a *stimulus* upon which you are required to respond.

In other words, we are positioned to choose how we are going to deal with adversity (i.e. guilt) stemming from the consequence of our actions, and how we choose to respond is determined by whether we are proactive or reactive in our thinking. This differentiation is especially important because each will produce vastly different consequences or results. The chain reaction principle is illustrated on the next page:

Chain Reaction Choice Model

CHOICE 1	CHOICE 2
STIMULUS	STIMULUS
	(Undesirable Consequence)
⇩	⇩
FREEDOM TO CHOOSE	FREEDOM TO CHOOSE
(Human Endowments)	(Human Endowments)
⇩	⇩
RESPONSE	RESPONSE
	(Reactive or Proactive)
⇩	⇩
CONSEQUENCE	CONSEQUENCE
(Undesirable)	(Undesirable or Desirable)

I indicated earlier that the Ghost of Guilt is summoned when we exercise our independent will and choose to respond in a way that contradicts what our conscience is telling us we *should do*. This is precisely what happens under "Choice 1" of the chain reaction model above when an undesirable consequence generates the depressive symptom of guilt. When you choose to respond to a stimulus that is in strict violation of your values, you create a void in your heart leading you to recognize that there is a *wrong that needs to be righted*. It follows that unless you fill this void with what your heart is telling you is the *right* thing to do, the void grows, as does the Ghost of Guilt.

The challenge, then, when burdened with guilt is to recognize that the chain reaction process provides an opportunity, a second chance if you will, to *right the wrong* that first occurred under the "Choice 1" response.

155

Alternatively, "Choice 2" provides an opportunity to fill the void which can serve to disempower the Ghost of Guilt.

The question is: how do we fill the void when you can't undo your mistake? I believe this question can be addressed by adopting Proactive Reconciliation Beliefs like those tabled earlier in the chapter, which requires first that we take full responsibility for our actions; and second, that we search to find meaning in our suffering (or guilt). On this footing, we are afforded the opportunity to not only learn from our perceived mistake, but leverage it to make us better.

I truly believe that there are important life lessons to be learned from consequences of a regretful "Choice 1" decision - lessons that can serve to strengthen character and encourage responsible decision making in the future. It is crucial to understand that the person you are (i.e. your character) is not determined by the perceived mistakes you make (in "Choice 1"), but rather, by how you respond to your mistakes (in "Choice 2").

I believe that when you discover value in suffering after making a mistake, you initiate proactive momentum in how you will respond to the "Choice 2" stimulus (i.e. the consequence from "Choice 1"). Being proactive in mind challenges limiting beliefs, and enables you to unweave that single, painful neurovegetative strand called guilt.

Suggestion: at this time, get a piece of paper (or return to your journal) and label a new page: "Step 3: Forgive myself." Find a quiet area, free from disruption, as the proactive reconciliation process that follows requires deep introspection by leveraging the endowments of awareness and imagination from the Proactive-Liberation Model for Depression.

Think for a moment and write down a specific stimulus or action in your life in which you responded in such a way that the resulting consequence produced a tremendous amount of guilt in your heart – and still does every time you think about it. Think of something that you feel that you've never truly moved on from, that you can't seem to forgive yourself for or find peace in.

This is a deep and very personal introspection exercise and as such, it is important to be proactive and willfully summon the Ghost of Guilt from this particular experience. Write it down and describe it in intimate detail so that you resurrect the associated painful emotions. When you complete this exercise, continue on and use the proactive reconciliation process that follows to help you learn to not only forgive yourself, but find meaning in your suffering.

UNWEAVE GUILT WITH PROACTIVE RECONCILIATION BELIEFS (PRBs)

The process of unweaving symptoms of depression requires that we leverage our human endowments in "Choice 2" of the Chain Reaction Choice Model in order to *respond proactively* and achieve a *desired consequence*. In the deep well context, this requires that we exert the conscious effort to release our grip on the Weeds of Damaging Beliefs (that which empowers *guilt*), and instead, embrace Proactive Reconciliation Beliefs to disempower and unweave this symptom of *guilt*.

In the proactive reconciliation process, we begin by first creating awareness and follow by leveraging the endowments of imagination and independent will to take the necessary action.

157

STEP 1: CREATE AWARENESS

The proactive reconciliation process begins in the "Choice 2" side of the Chain Reaction Choice Model. The very first step in this process may very well be the hardest to embrace because it requires that you strip your defenses and admit - not only to yourself, but to others - that you were *wrong* in how you chose to respond to the initial "Choice 1" stimulus in your life.

PRB #1: I Am Fully Responsible For My Actions

This means that you willfully take complete ownership of your actions and accept full responsibility for the resulting consequences, no matter how severe they are. This is the purest form of proactive thinking and is arguably the most unsettling because, in an emotional context, you must be willing to stand naked and exposed when having to face the consequences of your actions.

This means that by leveraging the endowment of self-awareness, you consciously strip away any reactively induced emotions (e.g. pride) and stop making excuses and blaming others or your conditions (e.g. personal circumstances, childhood, media, peer pressure, etc.) for how you chose to respond to the "Choice 1" stimulus.

By leveraging the endowment of conscience, you allow your heart to lead and determine what you need to do in order to *right the wrong* (i.e. that is, to respond appropriately to the "Choice 2" stimulus in order to achieve a desirable consequence). A proactive person in this respect willingly presents himself in a most vulnerable state, equipped with nothing more than a sincere heart, admission of wrongdoing, and a readiness to accept the consequences in full.

PRB #2: I Will Accept the Consequences

We experience undesirable consequences in our lives when we consciously make decisions that are in strict violation of our inner values and morals - the very components that form the human endowment of *conscience*. When we consciously adopt a proactive approach and accept full responsibility for our actions, we must then be prepared to take that deep breath and face the consequences.

Sometimes the choices we make can produce an undesirable consequence that reaches beyond *personal* condemnation (that which we can control), and spills over into the more fearful realm of *social* condemnation (which lies beyond our control). This concept is illustrated on the next page:

Relationship between Consequence and Condemnation

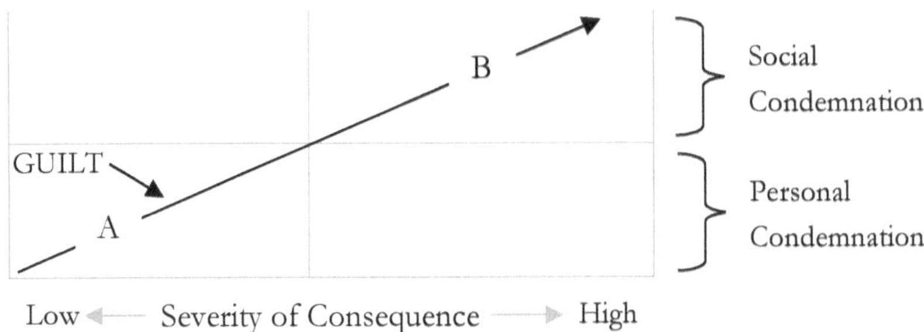

This graph serves to illustrate the direct relationship between the severity of a consequence and the associated condemnation that it may produce. Consider the following fictional scenario to illustrate: if I were to discreetly steal a five-dollar bill from someone's jacket at a house party and was the sole witness to my regretful action, then I would have to contend with the guilt associated with making a choice that was in strict violation of my personal values (i.e. believing that stealing is *wrong*). In this case, the severity of my consequence would lie on the "low" end of the scale, and the resulting condemnation would be contained in the personal condemnation quadrant (marked arbitrarily by point "A" on the graph above).

But what if someone saw me take that bill and confronted me publicly about it? The severity of my consequence therefore would increase because the associated condemnation spills over into the social quadrant which, unlike personal condemnation, cannot be controlled. The story about how I stole money would spread through the community like wildfire, and then I would be left to contend with not only my own personal condemnation, but that of society as well. The guilt associated with this regretful consequence would therefore increase into the social quadrant of condemnation (point "B" on the graph).

It is absolutely crucial to understand in this proactive reconciliation process for forgiving self that when you wholeheartedly and unconditionally choose to accept the consequences of your actions, you are exhibiting high *emotional intelligence*. This means that you consciously separate your *thoughts* from reactive, limiting emotions, and allow your *values* to set the course for how you will respond to the undesirable consequence (the stimulus in "Choice 2" of the Chain Reaction Choice Model).

This is an important step toward taking the opportunity to *right the wrong* generated from "Choice 1". The benefit to choosing this proactive approach when dealing with difficult consequences is that you stand to gain important life lessons, which not only serves to build character, but can position you to recognize value in making productive, value-based choices in the future. This is a benefit that can alleviate, to some degree, a guilt-ridden conscience in the *personal condemnation* quadrant above; however, in the *social* quadrant, it may not be as influential. This is because social condemnation, I believe, is embodied by *low* emotional intelligence.

Recognizing social condemnation for what it *really is*

I believe that the key to preserving one's integrity when subject to a socially condemning environment is to first recognize how superficial the social platform of condemnation truly is. Think about a time when you heard some shocking news about someone you know. Do you recall how you felt when you heard about what happened? Were you

161

overcome with disbelief? Did you feel excitement? Did you feel a sense of relief that it was this person experiencing the hardship and not you – with thoughts like *I'm glad it's him and not me!*?

When you heard this news, did you experience a sudden change in perception about the person in question? Did you immediately think less of his or her character? The next time you saw this person did you feel awkward in their presence? Did you think: *Oh my God. There she is?* Did you *look down on him* as a result of his actions? Do you remember whispering in contempt about them to another avid listener behind their back?

Be honest in your introspection exercise. Even though I am not proud to admit it, I know that these were some immediate reactions that I felt, and thought, when hearing about another's perceived downfall. There were times in my own life when I would stand amongst the masses, and in a figurative sense, cast stones of condemnation when a person was down and defenseless.

I have come to realize in healing that this type of behavior atop the platform of social condemnation was generated by low *emotional intelligence*.

Rising above social condemnation

It is important to understand the following logical distinction: when you admit your wrongdoing and willingly accept the consequences, you immediately begin to *right your wrong*. As a result, you stand to strengthen your character. This process, as you may appreciate, requires a high level of emotional intelligence.

On the other hand, when people condemn others for their actions, their response is driven by feelings, not values. As a result, they allow themselves to absorb limiting beliefs about that person serving only to *pull them down,* making them feel bad about themselves. This, in my opinion (and ironically), not only demonstrates lowness in character, but a lowness in emotional intelligence.

The point being: when you lay your heart on the line and prepare to accept the consequences of your regretful actions, *to right your wrong* if you will, then you are by virtue of higher character than those who, in a morbid sort of way, take pleasure from your suffering. I believe that you should never feel inferior to a condemning and reactive person because this would require that you, in a twist of irony, stoop to *their* level.

I believe there are three things to recognize to confidently rise above social condemnation created by an undesirable consequence: The first thing is recognizing that social blame is a mindless and reactive response that originates from low emotional intelligence. There is nothing proactive about social stigma because when a mass of distorted perceptions linger together, it forms a perverse cloud that serves only to depress the spirit and suffocate the soul.

The second is recognizing the emotional transition that reactive people experience when they choose to join the bandwagon of social condemnation. I call this *social-hypercritical metamorphosis:* it is the perceptive transformation that occurs in people when, at the expense of another person's suffering, they levitate to a sovereign hierarchy where they proclaim themselves grand judges of character and human worth. It is in this artificial dimension where people are judged by the extent to

163

which their actions violate the subjective – and sometimes hypocritical – moral code of the condemning person.

The third, and arguably the most important thing to recognize is that by following the proactive reconciliation process for guilt, I believe that social condemnation can be transformed into a more positive frame, like social acceptance or forgiveness. This is because people who stand on a social platform of condemnation are, by virtue, reactive in mind with low emotional intelligence. Actions of such people are determined by their emotions, which in turn are determined by their underlying beliefs or perceptions. By altering the perception of an emotionally <u>un</u>intelligent person, you can mechanically change the way they *feel* about a particular situation, or in this case, their perception about the undesirable consequence.

So how do we alter the perception of a condemning society? I believe that this can be done by a process of proactive introspection when answering the following questions: *what have I learned from my mistake, and how can this experience make me better?*

STEP 2: TAKE ACTION

Up to this point, we have created awareness through the proactive reconciliation process that we must be responsible for our actions and be willing to accept the consequences before we can learn to truly forgive ourselves. The next step is to put what we have learned into action.

This requires leveraging the endowment of imagination to extract lessons from painful, guilt-ridden experiences that we can leverage to make more proactive choices when faced with similar circumstances in the future. Such lessons might be represented by proclaiming a new system of value-based beliefs that serve to influence how we respond to similar situations in the future, such as: *I never want to feel that way again; I will never drink and drive again; I will never hit my spouse again;* and so on.

PRB #3: I Will Become Better Because of It

It is no secret that humans can learn to grow from making "mistakes." We can grow and become more knowledgeable in response to making choices that produce undesirable consequences and, ultimately, a guilty conscience. It is important to acknowledge that suffering can serve a purpose if you allow yourself to truly learn from it. It can serve as a valuable and necessary ingredient to your own personal growth and emotional development, and this in turn can benefit not only you personally, but others as well, particularly your family, friends and in time, your community.

In the words of Viktor Frankl, "…suffering ceases to be suffering at the moment it finds a meaning, such as the meaning of a sacrifice."[43]

I believe that the key to self-forgiveness or self-acceptance is finding meaning in your suffering from a guilt-ridden conscience. What is regarded as a regretful action or experience could otherwise be perceived as a sacrifice of oneself for the betterment of loved ones, who, in time, stand to benefit in life and in love because you suffered and sacrificed something.

To illustrate, I remember a conversation I had with my mother not too long after I was diagnosed with depression. She shared some very

165

painful childhood memories about her father, my late grandfather, whom I greatly admired growing up. I was quite surprised to hear of the strained relationship that existed between the two of them. My mother admitted to me that she hated him for many years and I realized that even in her late sixties, she remained haunted by these painful experiences, so much so that it still reduced her to tears when she talked about it.

I thought for a moment and in a proactive frame of mind, I told her something that immediately altered her perception about this painful experience in her life:

"There was never a time in my life when I ever said 'I hate my mother.'"

"I should hope not!" she responded. "I did everything I could to make sure you and your sister had a better life than I did."

So I challenged her:

"Do you see what happened here? You learned in your suffering that you would never treat your children the way you were treated. In other words, you learned to be a better parent relative to how you perceived your father was to you. You raised your children differently and in such a way that they never learned to hate their mother. You must realize that it is because of your sacrifice that you provided a better home life for your children and this is why you should instead view your painful memories with honor and dignity."

My mother was speechless. After a long pause, lost in her own contemplation, she told me that she had never thought about it that way before. After we hung up, I felt that she was able to truly find value in her suffering and this proactive perspective eased the emotional grip it had on her heart for so many years.

PRB #4: I Will 'Pay It Forward' (Help Others)

The final Proactive Reconciliation Belief is taking what you have learned from an undesirable consequence (i.e. "Choice 1" of the chain reaction choice model) and putting it into action in such a way that it stands to benefit others. I believe that the key to self-forgiveness is to re-establish personal worth or value in oneself by taking the proactive initiative to *right the wrong*, by doing whatever it takes to fill the void in your heart.

When you pay it forward, you demonstrate not only to yourself, but to others as well, that although you are truly remorseful for your actions, you are striving to learn from your mistakes and be better. You demonstrate that you are prepared to sacrifice part of yourself in order to *give back* what others may perceive you *took away* by your initial response. It is through this process of making a difference in another life where you stand to discover meaning and purpose in your own suffering, while at the same time disempowering the hurtful, consequential effects that radiate from social condemnation.

When you *pay it forward*, you create a gust of momentum, which in time stands to alter its course, redirecting it onto a more productive pathway toward social forgiveness or acceptance. When you demonstrate to others by your tireless effort to *right the wrong* you have caused, you stand to contradict the damaging beliefs of emotionally reactive beings from which social condemnation cultivates. Subsequently, you stand to mechanically alter their superficial perceptions toward a more positive realm of acceptance.

167

APPLYING THE PROACTIVE RECONCILIATION PROCESS FOR GUILT

The following scenario is inspired by a real-life incident; however, the facts have been altered to respect the privacy of those involved.

To illustrate this proactive reconciliation process for guilt, I am going to make reference to a tragic car accident that occurred a number of years ago which, at the hands of an impaired driver, resulted in the passing of someone I knew. I genuinely believe that this reconciliation process can be applied to even the most tragic of circumstances, such as this one in which I was indirectly, yet personally affected.

The driver of the vehicle, whom I will refer to as "John," made a decision one fateful day to drive home from a party. He struck an oncoming vehicle, killing the driver. Although I have never met John, I can only imagine the heaviness that he must carry in his heart every waking day of his life. The Ghost of Guilt that spawned from that tragic day must be incredibly overwhelming. It is logical to suggest that at some point in this dreadful experience, John believed: *I will never forgive myself for that.*

The proactive reconciliation process that follows is written as if John were reading this right now, hoping to find liberation from depressive symptoms and wishing he could learn to forgive himself for his tragic mistake. More specifically, it is written as a means to help John recognize that he can learn to truly forgive himself. More importantly, he will learn to identify that there is meaning in his suffering and that his victim's death does not have to be regarded in vain.

PRB #1: I Am Fully Responsible For My Actions

In this scenario, John would have to step outside of himself and be consciously prepared to strip away his defenses before he could begin to forgive himself for what he had done. By reactive thinking, he could try to convince himself that it wasn't his fault, that it was because he was drinking, or his friends convinced him to go, or the sun was in his eyes, and so on. But deep down inside, his heart knows the truth (i.e. conscience) and until he is willing to accept full responsibility for choosing to get behind the wheel of his vehicle that fateful day, his conscience will remain guilt-ridden and he will be forever haunted by the Ghost of Guilt. The first step toward forgiving self in this example is for John to accept unconditional responsibility for his actions and accept the fact that he made a personal choice that resulted in the tragic death of another human being. The next step for John is to be prepared to fully accept the consequences of his actions.

PRB #2: I Will Accept the Consequences

John could contemplate through the endowment of awareness how the tragic consequence of his actions impacted not only his own family, but the victim's as well; his friends, as well as the victim's circle of friends; his workplace, as well as the victim's workplace; and the community in which they both resided. The exercise of *putting yourself in someone else's shoes* can be a painful and overwhelming exercise because it extends far beyond the borders of his immediate social circle – including distant relatives, friends, co-workers, community, and so on.

Every day, John would be vulnerable to social condemnation for what he did to the victim and the victim's family. He could also have been

169

condemned by those close to him for bringing shame to his family. The societal mistreatment can be in the form of direct verbal and physical mistreatment, or in an indirect form, like attacking his character behind his back. John would stand to face public scrutiny every time he left his house, wherever he would go. Regardless, John is left with negative perceptions or beliefs of how he thinks people perceive his character and this can produce a tremendous amount of mental and emotional anguish, which in turn can erode his perception of self-worth.

PRB #3: I Will Become Better Because of It

John has to believe that even though he may wish that he *could* go back in time and change his fateful choice, to <u>not</u> get into his vehicle and drive home, it is an unproductive exercise. I believe it hinders any proactive attempt to coping and healing. Alternatively, John could instead face his fear, summon the Ghost of Guilt from that fateful accident, and discover things that he can learn from that regretful experience to make him better. Perhaps he may recognize the negative association he now feels about drinking alcohol and refuse to touch another drop in his life. This single decision could have an enormous positive influence on his life, possibly enabling him to be a better husband, father and citizen. Alternatively, under a reactive frame of mind, he may choose to absorb himself in the past and succumb to the debilitating effect of guilt, which he may deal with by excessive drinking. This decision, as you can imagine, would also stand to have a profound effect on his future.

PRB #4: I Will 'Pay It Forward' (Help Others)

By leveraging the Proactive-Liberation Model for Depression, John could form the belief that *no one should ever live with the painful emotions that I have had to experience since the accident* and put into action a plan to help educate people on the dangers of drinking and driving. His personal convictions could turn him off alcohol, and he could choose instead to leverage lessons from this tragic experience to shape the rest of his life. On the social platform, he could leverage his convictions and form partnerships with other educational networks, such as Mothers Against Drunk Driving (MADD) and Students Against Drinking and Driving (SADD). He could share with people his own disturbing and tragic experiences in hopes of deterring others from making the same terrible choice that he had made.

These are examples of proactive measures that John could adopt in his own life that, in time, could alter not only his own perception of self, but also the damaging perceptions from social condemnation. It is when society sees that you are reaching out and striving to be better that they subconsciously process an alternate perspective that you are demonstrating *to them* true repentance for your actions (i.e. they see that you are giving back and *paying it forward*). Social *condemnation* then converges into social *acceptance*. The few who witness John's proactive measures can greatly influence the social perception of the masses which again, speaks to the superficiality that underlies social condemnation.

FORGIVING SELF

What truly matters then is the spiritual and emotional transformation that occurs intimately within the self. This occurs deep within your heart when you achieve surreal and personal fulfillment that comes from reaching out and making a difference in the lives of others. It could be personally focused, such as learning from difficult experiences to be a better spouse or parent, or it could be socially focused, such as educating the public and trying to save others from making the same regretful choices.

In John's case, he could learn from this tragic experience to become a better husband, parent and citizen. He could learn to not take his family for granted because such a consequence could happen to anyone, thus establishing more loving and meaningful relationships. In a proactive context, he could grow tremendously as a person and, by establishing a higher moral standard in his life, could have an invaluable influence on the lives of others and society in general. That is, in a proactive context, he could learn to accept himself for the better person that he has the opportunity to become. By proactive reconciliation, he will have discovered meaning in his suffering, and through personal growth and helping others, he could fill the void in his heart because the death he had caused would no longer have to be regarded in vain, but rather, as a life force owing to the betterment of himself, his family and society.

In the words of Viktor E. Frankl: In some way, suffering ceases to be suffering at the moment it finds a meaning, such as the meaning of a sacrifice."[44]

Ladder of Liberation Step 3: Action Steps to Forgive Self

1.   Take full responsibility for your actions

Be willing to lay down your defenses, take ownership and accept responsibility for your actions. How you respond to *negative* experiences in your life will define who you are and the type of person you will become. View these experiences as "necessary ingredients" that will shape the person you are today and will be tomorrow.

2.   Prepare to accept the consequences of your actions

Be prepared to accept the consequences of your actions, unconditionally. Through proactive reconciliation, acknowledge that you stand above social condemnation for what truly is a reactive and harmful conduct that is supported by low emotional intelligence. Associate with those who truly care for you and who will reserve judgment for your actions. You want to surround yourself with people who are prepared to stand by your side during the most difficult times. These people are proactive in mind and will be there to lift you up while others, through social condemnation, attempt to pull you down.

3.   Learn how you can become better from this experience

Through introspection, look inside yourself and connect with the painful emotions that stem from your regretful experience. Feel them intimately and use these painful emotions as motivation by declaring that you never want to feel this way again when faced with similar circumstances in the future. Use imagination and project how you would respond differently (proactively) in the future if ever faced with the same type of stimulus or action again. Reconnect with your inner values and morals and acknowledge that you have learned a valuable lesson from this experience and that you will be better because of it.

173

4.   Take what you have learned and "pay it forward"

Discover how you can take the valuable lessons learned from your regretful experience and use this information to not only improve your own life, but others as well. Be selfless with your productive knowledge and reach out and share your intimate experiences with other people or groups. By being proactive and learning how to improve the lives of others by giving a piece of yourself – that is, by sharing your personal experiences - you can discover meaning and purpose in your suffering, and truly make a difference.

CHAPTER 12

Action Step #4: Create a Goal

The Chain Reaction Choice Model presented in Chapter 11 has important implications with respect to how life in general is perceived. I believe that this can help shape a more proactive belief system when it comes to healing in depression. The illustration presented on the next page is what I call the *Timeline of Life Model* and serves to represent my perception of life as it *happens*.

Timeline of Life Model

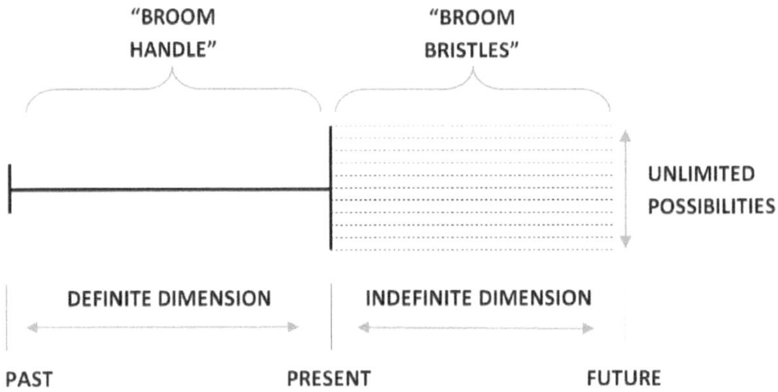

I liken my timeline of life concept to that of a broom: the "handle" is represented by the time period that separates the past from the present, and the "bristles" of the broom symbolize a future that is uncertain and full of possibilities.

THE DEFINITE DIMENSION ("BROOM HANDLE")

A closer inspection of the broom handle would reveal that it is shaped by the succession of past choices and decisions made in life. This means that every decision that you have ever made throughout the course of every waking hour creates the pathway that links your past to your present reality. Furthermore, since time is a fixed measure, the *pathway* is represented by a straight line (labeled "definite dimension" in the diagram). Every experience that you have ever encountered in your life, whether perceived positively or negatively, forms a single stepping stone on the *historic pathway* leading up to your *today*. Although we exist in our present reality, we can utilize the innate endowments of self-awareness

176

and imagination to go back in time and revisit – or in figurative terms – *stand on* any one stepping stone of our past. Conceptually speaking, when you observe from a distance the countless number of stepping stones that line up to our present state, it takes the shape of a broom handle.

THE INDEFINITE DIMENSION ("BROOM BRISTLES")

The indefinite dimension in the Timeline of Life Model simply represents the future - an extension of our timeline that is not yet defined. Our future is determined by the same way we cement our past with stepping stones: by the *choices* we make. The indefinite dimension is illustrated by "broom bristles" which are attached to the figurative "broom handle" of our past. For example, one bristle might represent a sequence of choices that creates a future pathway in your life with more education and a fulfilling career. Alternatively, another bristle might represent a sequence of alternate choices that creates a less flattering pathway such as going to prison as a consequence of a regretful choice. These bristles serve to symbolize a future with unlimited possibilities.

This is an important distinction in the context of depression because although our recent past may have been burdened by this disorder, it is not *destined* to continue into the future unless you choose to allow it. As you should now be fully aware, because you own the freedom to make choices in your life in your present, you therefore possess the power to shape your future.

177

PROACTIVE 180 DEGREE REFOCUS

The indefinite dimension in the timeline of life model shares one single, but vastly important characteristic with the definite dimension: *time travel*. That is, just like we can utilize the innate endowments of self-awareness and imagination in our present reality to go back and revisit a past experience, we can also leverage these same endowments to project ourselves into the future and envision pathways of unchartered territory.

To truly heal in depression, I believe, requires a dynamic shift in mental focus – a one hundred and eighty degree turn from the *reactive*, definite dimension, to the *proactive*, indefinite dimension. This transition requires that we first stop living in the past; and second, we learn to reconnect with our inner spirit to create a future goal that we can aspire to.

Transitional Step 1:
Stop Living In The Past

The transitional step: *stop living in the past*, was difficult for me to accept in my healing because it requires that we sever the deep emotional strings that keeps pulling us back in time to a particular "stepping stone," upon which we relive a guilt-ridden experience. On this stone, I would feel terribly overwhelmed, burdened by what I perceived was a regretful choice. This, in turn, would fuel depressive symptoms like hopelessness and worthlessness. I would linger in this reactive frame, wishing I could somehow go back in time and undo what I perceived was a *wrong* in my life.

Applying the proactive reconciliation process for guilt (described in chapter 11) enabled me to loosen and sever these emotionally restraining strings. By taking full responsibility for my actions, accepting the consequences, learning to be better, and finding meaning and purpose in my suffering, I learned to forgive and accept not only myself, but others whose actions may have contributed to such painful memories.

Establishing a base of proactive beliefs can serve to add considerable leverage when trying to let go of the past so you can instead focus on the future. Below are three such beliefs which I have personally adopted in my own life:

1) Things happen as a matter of consequence
2) I don't perceive my choices as either "right" or "wrong"
3) I can't change the past and nor would I want to

1.   Things happen as a matter of consequence

This proactive belief directly contradicts the more common belief that *things happen for a reason*, which implies that the consequence that stems from our freedom of choice model is influenced by an unnatural force, one typically associated with religious belief. My interpretation of this is that life is seemingly preplanned for you, and our future pathways predetermined. The bumps along the way (i.e. life's challenges) are typically part of a divine plan as you progress toward your *set* destination, wherever that might be.

I personally believe that the things that happen in my life, past or present, occur as a matter of consequence from the choices that I make. This proactive belief is predicated on the stimulus-response choice

179

model from the previous chapter which recognizes our innate human freedom to choose our response. In turn, our freedom to choose extends to how we respond to resulting consequences. This human condition of choice is what enables humans the ability to grow and advance, to be proactive and responsible in life.

2.   I don't perceive my choices as either "right" or "wrong"

I have come to the realization throughout my experience with depression – through research and consultations with my psychiatrist – that there is no universal definition of *right* and *wrong* when having to answer to life's questions. Rather, there are only *consequences* of choice.

This might be perceived as a highly controversial statement to make but it is one that I wholeheartedly believe in. Because of this, I have been able to disempower certain emotional strings which otherwise would constrain me when dwelling on what I would perceive were "wrong" decisions in my life. You will notice throughout this book that affirmations such as *right* and *wrong* are expressed in italics because of this proactive, but controversial, belief. This is because what is considered *right* and what is considered *wrong* is personal and subjective to each individual (perhaps by selective interpretation), and therefore, not universally defined (irrespective of social laws). For example, we can all likely agree that killing a person is *wrong*! In fact, this is one of the Ten Commandments in the Bible. However, interpretations will change depending on the circumstances. If a person points a gun at someone and gets shot down and killed by police, is the act of killing *wrong* in this instance? Or is it justifiably *right*? The point is (barring further philosophical debate), what is *right* and what is *wrong* is not etched in stone – no pun intended.

In the timeline of life model, particularly in the definite dimension, we are where we are today because of the sequence of choices that we have made in the past. Throughout life, we will respond to challenges in ways that will produce both desirable and undesirable consequences, but regardless of how these are perceived, each choice that we make forms a single stepping stone that extends the pathway leading from our past to our present. Each stone along this pathway offers a constructive learning opportunity that we can leverage to help grow and be better should we *choose* to do so. When we do, we can look back on decisions we have made in the past, not with guilt or regret, or with reactive notions of *right* or *wrong*, but rather as necessary factors owing to our personal growth and development.

This train of thought complements the term "blessing in disguise" because when we look back on what we once perceived was a "wrong" or "regretful" choice, but have learned to become better as a result, then the perception of that choice is no longer a question of being *wrong* or *right*. Instead, it can be viewed with a proactive lens as being necessary and purposeful.

3.   I can't change the past and nor would I want to

As I described earlier in this chapter, every past experience in your life, whether perceived positively or negatively, forms a permanent stepping stone along the pathway of life that links the past to the present. The obvious reality is that we cannot go back in time and change the past even though we may quite often fantasize about doing so, with thoughts like *if I could do it all over again, I would do it differently this time!* This is a very reactive and unproductive perspective or belief about a specific past experience that serves only to generate in our present reality, pain or guilt.

This means that you have not effectively dealt with your past issues and have yet to extract from these painful experiences meaning and purpose. The key point here is that you fail to recognize the potentially valuable life lessons your past experiences offer you – lessons that stand to improve your life in the future by making you better today. This is the reason why I would never want to go back in time to change things, even if I could.

I would not be the man I am today without having suffered first, and I would not have suffered without having made regretful choices in my past. Without having experienced the pain, guilt and other incapacitating symptoms of depression, I would not have discovered purpose in my life, which is to help people heal in depression. In addition, I would not have had the opportunity to create a future goal to strive for, which for me, is to publish this very book you are holding in your hands.

Transitional Step 2:
Create A Future Goal To Look Forward To

The second step that I believe is required to complete the dynamic shift in mental focus, from the *reactive*, definite dimension to the *proactive*, indefinite dimension, is to create a future goal to strive for. On his prison life experience, Viktor Frankl indicated that prisoners who chose to live in the past deprived themselves of the opportunities to learn and grow from their present difficulties. He stated that in the absence of a future goal, life for these prisoners became meaningless. The principle of finding a future goal, then, is to instill meaning in one's life, to provide a reason or desire to move forward, or in the figurative context, to keep climbing. Following a proactive 180 degree refocus, from the past and toward a future goal, the timeline of life model can be simplified as illustrated below:

Timeline of Life Model: Creating a Future Goal

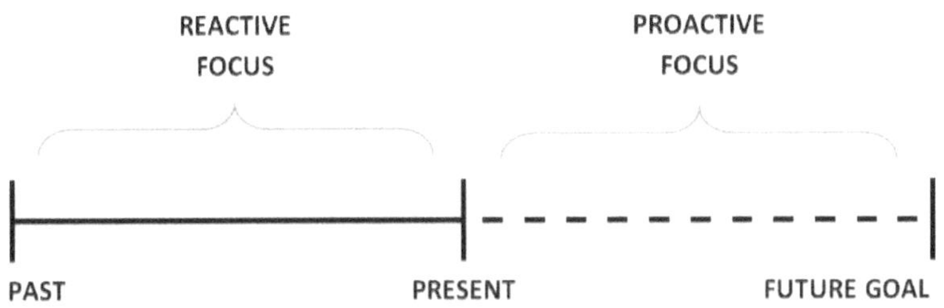

Living in the past produces reactive implications for the future because when our sights are pointed behind us, we are not focused on where we are heading. The past is a fixed element along the timeline of life model, while the future is variable, determined only by the choices we make in our present.

When in our present reality we remain reactively consumed by our past, the future becomes subconsciously neglected. On the timeline of life model, our future blindly passes us by and becomes something that just happens to us as we casually drift through the motions of life.

Proactive focus

I believe that when you identify a future goal to strive for, you have effectively isolated a single "bristle" from the unlimited spectrum of future possibilities, determined by your perception of what would be a desirable outcome for your life. This "broom bristle" is representative of

183

the sequence of choices that are available to you throughout the proactive process of striving for a future goal.

Refocus and liberation

I believe that we complete the proactive 180 degree refocus process when two conditions are met: first, a future goal is clearly defined, and second, the journey towards achieving it is put into motion. Establishing a future goal to aspire to requires deep introspection, a *soul-searching* exercise if you will, to discover your inner passion. This dictates what it is you truly want to accomplish in your life.

It is something that creates a surge of excitement every time you think about it. It is something that keeps you up at night and gets you out of bed in the morning, as you tirelessly strive to achieve it. You are driven in your pursuit of achieving your goal by an intense emotional connection to it. Defining a goal in your life to look forward to is a proactive exercise of awareness; however, unless it is acted upon, it quickly materializes into a reactive and static dream which can ultimately cause *frustration of the heart*. This happens when you consciously resist the direction your heart wants you to move in.

The second condition for completing the proactive 180 degree refocus exercise is to act on achieving your goal. When the wheels are in motion, so to speak, you can produce tremendous momentum with respect to unweaving certain symptoms of depression. This is because of the constructive implications associated with proactively pursuing a goal: firstly, you cannot live in the past while you point your sights forward because you cannot focus on both directions simultaneously. Therefore, you generate empowering and productive emotions when focused on the future and alleviate depressive symptoms generated by living in the past. This enables you to exercise a proactive frame of mind which in turn can produce considerable leverage when having to make value-based decisions in response to life's challenges.

Secondly, you stand to build momentum when striving to reach your goal by leveraging what I call *proactive association*: the act of associating with proactive-minded individuals who are already where you want to be. Surrounding yourself with like-minded people can serve as a tremendous source of motivation and encouragement as you strive to accomplish whatever it is you are aspiring for. Most importantly, you also stand to gain tremendous leverage in your healing in the deep well context by adding to your existing network of supporters who have gripped in hand your Rope of Support.

"REFOCUS" IN PERSPECTIVE

Creating a future goal to strive for generates proactive and productive emotions like hope, fulfillment and self-worth. In turn, this can serve to alleviate, by some measure, depressive symptoms. I believe that the key to achieving liberation from this disorder is to be consciously proactive and consistent in your refocusing efforts. This may require setting a multitude of smaller goals to build momentum as you strive to achieve your primary goal.

Ladder of Liberation Step 4: Action Steps to Create a Goal

1. Stop living in the past

Accept the reality that you cannot change the past. However, acknowledge that you can learn valuable life lessons from it and that you can leverage these lessons to make proactive decisions as you define your future. Challenge your belief system with proactive assertions. For example, when troubled by a hurtful memory from your past, realize that these particular life experiences are necessary components that owe to your personal growth and emotional development. Recognize that what you may perceive are regretful mistakes should actually be viewed as valuable life lessons that can bless you with the wisdom to make more proactive-driven choices in your life – which, in turn, can produce a more hopeful future. Further, I believe you must learn to recognize that "suffering" is really a "sacrifice" and when you perceive your sacrifice as giving a piece of yourself for the betterment of others, you will enrich your life with meaning and purpose. This, in turn, can create positive ripple effects that extend far beyond yourself, affecting family, friends and society in general.

2. Take an inventory of your strengths and passions

Leverage awareness and conscience to find answers to proactive questions such as: what am I good at or passionate about? What is it that I could do that would generate fulfillment in my life? What am I enthusiastic about? What is it that would keep me up late at night and get me out of bed early in the morning? This exercise requires a deep level of introspection, a soul-searching exercise if you will, which requires acute attention to what your heart is telling you. Write down everything your heart is dictating and think about how you can use these proactive attributes to create a goal to aspire to.

3. *Create a goal and make a deadline to achieve it*

Leverage imagination and project yourself into the future at some point along the timeline of life and envision yourself actually achieving your goal. See yourself where it is that you truly want to be in your life. Determine at what point on the timeline you *need* to achieve your goal and this will provide the hunger or sense of urgency to accomplish it on time. On whatever "broom bristle" that you have identified as an ideal path for your future, begin by setting small, achievable goals to build momentum as you strive to reach your ultimate goal.

4. *Develop relationships with people who can help you achieve your goal*

When you determine where it is you want to be in your life, be proactive and reach out to people who are already where it is that you want to be. Find a mentor, someone who will provide you with the focus, motivation and encouragement you need throughout your journey. A mentor will hold you accountable as you work to achieve your goal. A mentor is someone who will never give up on you until you consciously choose to give up on yourself. This will be nearly impossible to do when you are accountable to someone who truly wants you to succeed in your life as they have in their own.

187

CHAPTER 13

Action Step #5: Exercise to Heal

"A review of studies stretching back to 1981 concluded that regular exercise can improve mood in people with mild to moderate depression. It also may play a supporting role in treating severe depression."[45]

The steps leading up to this fifth rung on the Ladder of Liberation require that we challenge how we think about depression. The knowledge and perspectives up to this point position us to effectively leverage a more proactive belief system that enables us to seek help, forgive ourselves, and refocus on life. This chapter aims to complement our proactive mindset with the direct physiological and psychological benefits that come from regular physical exercise.

It is crucial to understand at this stage in our journey that the treatment of depression is not limited to psychological means, but rather, is effectively influenced by physical means as well. The underlying message is that we not only need to be proactive in mind, but I believe we must also be proactive in body to successfully achieve liberation from the Deep Well of Depression.

When I was treading water in this context, life, for me, felt incredibly overwhelming. I believed that I was failing in almost every area of my life, burdened constantly by what I perceived was a long history of regretful choices and difficult consequences. These limiting perceptions generated tremendous stress in my daily life which, over time, snowballed into bigger anxieties until I had reached my breaking point.

These psychological stresses not only served to erode my mental health, but produced very real physical symptoms in my body, such as: upset stomach and nausea, insomnia (difficulty falling asleep) and fatigue, heart palpitations and difficulty breathing, frequent sickness, and so on. These were immediate physical consequences resulting either directly or indirectly from prolonged exposure to stressful conditions.

What I did not take into consideration at the time were the potential long term health consequences by continuing down this path. It was not until I began to research *how* psychological stress affects the body's physiological functioning that I truly felt a sense of urgency to be proactive and do everything in my power to improve both my mental and physical health.

189

ESTABLISHING A PROACTIVE PERSPECTIVE OF EXERCISE

The foremost purpose of this chapter is to establish a *proactive perspective of exercise* in the mindset of a person struggling with depression. I personally understand that this can be a very difficult task, especially when overwhelmed with certain symptoms. However, speaking from my own personal struggles, it is a very crucial step toward healing, so much so that it serves as an essential rung on the Ladder of Liberation.

Exercise produces direct physiological and psychological benefits that can serve to reduce the perception of pain in the body and elevate mood, creating a positive perception of mind. These naturally-produced benefits provide tremendous leverage in our goal of healing in depression, but again, they can only be realized when we make that conscious choice to be proactive and engage in regular physical activity when faced with painful symptoms.

A Three-Staged Approach

I have identified throughout my journey in this disorder three fundamental stages to establishing a proactive perspective of exercise when faced with depressive symptoms:

Stage 1: Create awareness

The first stage requires that we learn and become consciously aware of what is actually happening in our bodies when subject to debilitating symptoms. This further requires understanding about why we feel the way we do in this disorder, and being conscious of the inherent, longer-term health risks associated with being *reactive* in our approach to responding to symptoms.

Stage 2: Embrace the science

The second stage requires that we establish a resounding argument in support of the very real physiological and therapeutic benefits of physical exercise. This further requires that we acknowledge exercise as a potentially powerful alternative to taking medication for the treatment of depression.

Stage 3: Move on it

The third stage requires that we take what we have learned from the first two stages, and put it into motion. By leveraging our human endowments, we learn in this stage how to apply a proactive perspective of exercise.

STAGE 1: CREATE AWARENESS (WHAT IS HAPPENING TO MY BODY?)

"Understanding the way our bodies work in response to our thoughts validates the importance of being proactive, rather than just reactive, in coping with the effects of stress."[46]

This section provides a general overview of the science behind how the human body responds to depressive symptoms and stress. The link between chronic stress and depression is also identified and discussed.

Key points to be taken from this section are listed below and serve as the primary subject headings for the content that follows:

- The body has a built-in stress response system to deal with acute (physical) stress conditions;
- The body (or its natural stress response system) is not designed to effectively deal with chronic (psychological) stress conditions;
- The body emits warning signals in response to chronic stress;
- Depression is one of many serious health consequences associated with chronic stress;
- To heal in depression, we must strive for balance in our psychological and physiological capacities.

The Body Has a Built-In Stress Response System

In their book *Stress Management for Life*, the authors[47] explain the physiology and psychology of stress, stating that the human body is naturally programmed to respond to perceived threats and dangers that we experience throughout the course of our lives.

This programming is a primitive trait in humans and the authors explain it in the context of what is referred to as a "Fight-or-Flight" response, represented by "…a surge of physiological processes (that) floods the body automatically and precisely."[48] In modern society, the human body's stress response mechanism (i.e. "fight-or-flight" response) is triggered by threats that are typically physical in nature, such as childbirth, natural disasters, attacks by animals or people, a car accident (or a close call), a heart attack, and so on. These are all examples of *acute stress* situations, and the authors explain that the "…demand, danger or threat is quick, immediate, very real, and usually does not last very long."[49]

Consider the following example for illustrative purposes: imagine yourself walking down a sidewalk, enjoying a relaxing stroll. Suddenly, out of nowhere, a dog ferociously charges towards you. In an instant, your body falls into a state of shock. Whether you are aware or not, your primitive instincts kick in. If you were alone, then your body might instinctively respond by running away from this creature (i.e. take "flight"); or if you were walking with a child, your body might instinctively respond by confronting this animal in order to protect your child (i.e. "fight"). The authors state that the only purpose of this "built-in" stress response mechanism is to help us survive what we perceive to be threats and dangers.

In this situation, the "shock" sensation that the body would experience is what the authors explain "…is a state of physiological and psychological hyperarousal. The cascade of nervous system activity and

193

release of stress hormones lead to immediate responses that help a person deal with danger…"[50]

How the Stress Response System Is Regulated

The stress response in the human body is regulated by two branches of the nervous system: the sympathetic and parasympathetic nervous systems.

The SNS activates the stress response in the body

The sympathetic nervous system (SNS) is responsible for turning the stress response mechanism in the body to the "on" position, meaning that it initiates the stress response and "shocks" the body to prepare it for the perceived threat.

The authors[51] identify a number of these physiological changes that take place in the body during this period of hyperarousal: it first begins with a discharge of hormones, particularly adrenaline (or epinephrine), noradrenaline (or norepinephrine) and a steroid hormone called cortisol. Collectively, these hormones facilitate the stress response system and are responsible for increasing heart rate and cardiac output, blood pressure, and redirecting blood flow and glucose (the primary source of energy) to muscles in preparation for physical response (i.e. fight or run).

This surge of physiological resources to the muscles helps to explain how a person can exhibit seemingly abnormal bouts of strength and speed in a life or death situation. For this to happen however, the authors explain that other important functions of the body become suppressed when blood flow and energy are diverted to systems that support physical survival: the immune system, reproductive system, digestive system, and excretory system are all suppressed when the SNS is activated in response to a perceived threat.

The PNS de-activates the stress response system

The authors[52] explain that the parasympathetic nervous system (PNS) is responsible for turning the stress response mechanism to the "off" position, meaning it is responsible for returning the body back to a balanced state of functioning (i.e. a state of *homeostasis*) after the perceived threat or danger has passed. The PNS is responsible for "undoing" the physiological processes initiated by SNS activity in response to the perceived threat.

A considerable amount of energy is required by the PNS to reduce the presence of stress hormones in the body after its initial surge, and redirect blood flow and glucose back to bodily systems that were temporarily suppressed by way of SNS activity. This correction process therefore can result in physical exhaustion after the perceived threat has passed.

The body's stress response system is designed to help a person survive a perceived danger by effectively preparing the body to fight or run. This is aided by a complex series of physiological processes that, according to the authors, is usually quick, immediate and does not last long.

A question: what if the perceived danger is *not* a product of acute stress, but rather of a psychological or social nature? Alternatively, how does our body respond to worries and anxieties related to non-physical

195

threats such as financial problems, workplace stress, arguments, relationship breakdowns, death of a loved one, and so on?

The authors make reference to two very important characteristics of the stress response system in human beings that addresses these questions. First, "…our bodies are unable to distinguish between life-threatening dangers and more mundane problems such as a disagreement (or)…debt…" and second, "You only need to 'think' you are in danger for the stress response to activate."[53]

The body does not process chronic stress effectively

One important implication with respect to the first characteristic is that this stress response mechanism in humans ("fight-or-flight") is the only defense mechanism available to the body to respond to modern day stresses, whether they are acute stress situations or psychological.

One size does *not* fit all, so to speak. Research supports that the body's stress response system is designed to respond effectively and efficiently to *acute* stress situations, but does not respond effectively to *psychological* threats. In an acute stress situation for example, the perceived threat is determined by an external or physical stimulus, a circumstance that is likely beyond your control (such as a dog attacking). The physiological result, as we have learned, is instinctive and immediate. The perception of a threat stimulates the central nervous system which activates the stress response.

The threat in an acutely stressful situation is generally quick and does not last long, causing the central nervous system to turn the stress response "off" after the perceived threat has subsided. In this example,

196

the attacking dog - or the external stimulus - would be identified as the root cause of the perceived threat that subsequently led to a surge of physiological processes in the body.

Threat Is Internalized

In psychological stress conditions, the perceived threat is *not* determined by a physical stimulus. Rather, it is generated internally, by how we perceive the particular experience we are faced with. That is, we *create* the threat in our minds, which in turn, stimulates the nervous system and activates the stress response (as though there actually was an imminent physical threat).

Recall the first characteristic above: "…our bodies are unable to distinguish between life-threatening dangers and more mundane problems…"[54] Furthermore, it follows then that because we are responsible for *creating* the threat, then by logic, we must be responsible for *dismantling* it before the body can achieve balance. It is when we fail to deal with our perceived threats effectively that prevents the central nervous system from returning the body to its balanced state.

So what all of this means is that the stress response system remains in the "on" position due to the inability of the nervous system (or more specifically, the PNS) to turn it "off." The authors[55] link this malfunction of the stress response system to what is referred to as *chronic stress*. This is key to understanding not only why the stress response system is inadequate to handle psychological stress, but more significantly, how chronic stress can manifest into sickness and disease.

197

The body's warning signs of chronic stress

I've since learned in my research that the slow regression of my mental health was indicative of what is called the "General Adaptation Syndrome"[56]. In simple terms, this is the body trying to function normally in an otherwise abnormal state due to its inability to return to homeostasis.

The authors[57] explain that when this happens, the stress response system stays "on", but operates at a reduced level of hyperarousal. Over time, the body begins to *adapt* to this state of physiological imbalance which can result in abnormal bodily functioning and eventual break-down. I liken the general adaptation syndrome to that of consciously driving a car while its engine light flashes, indicating that there is a problem with its internal mechanical system. By consistently ignoring the warning signal, it would just be a matter of time before the engine breaks down completely.

Our bodies operate in the same manner: if we choose to ignore the warning signals that chronic stress emits in our bodies, then it is just a matter of time before our physical and mental health deteriorates.

So it follows then - what are the warning signals of chronic stress? My research on the physiological consequences of stress has helped me to not only identify the common symptoms in the body, but understand *why* I was feeling the way I was throughout my struggle with depression.

Signs of Chronic Stress

In the book *Stress Management for Life*, the authors[58] identify some common (and immediate) signs of chronic stress and explain their associated physiological responses, which I have summarized below:

Upset stomach

When the stress response is activated, the digestive system becomes suppressed as blood flow is redirected from the digestive tract to the muscles and limbs (preparing the body for the "fight or flight" response). This results in continued muscle contraction. A suppressed digestive system makes it difficult to break down and absorb food effectively. This produces a "knotting" or upset stomach sensation when feeling stressed.

Lying awake at night

The simple task of going to bed for a good night's sleep can become difficult when the mind is racing with worrisome and stressful thoughts. As indicated earlier, the body's stress response system is activated by simply thinking about a perceived threat. When this happens, the body responds by releasing adrenaline hormones which causes the mind to be aroused and alert instead of calm and relaxed, therefore making it difficult to fall asleep.

Fatigue and soreness

Chronic stress not only makes it difficult to get to sleep, but it can disrupt sleep patterns throughout the night leading to sleep deprivation and fatigue. When the body's stress response does not turn off under chronic stress conditions, it expends a tremendous amount of energy (glucose) to keep muscles contracted for a prolonged period of time –

ready to fight or take flight. This can result in muscle tension and soreness.

Increased heart rate

Activation of the stress response results in increased secretion of adrenaline in the body, which leads to an accelerated heart rate and shortness of breath. Again, under chronic stress conditions, this is the body's natural response to fight or take flight, even though no imminent physical threat exists.

Frequent sickness

The immune system is another important function of the body that becomes suppressed when the SNS is activated in response to stress. In simple terms, the immune system protects the body from disease and sickness, so prolonged exposure to chronic stress weakens the body's natural defense mechanism.

These were some common symptoms of chronic stress and anxiety that I lived with throughout my depression. In retrospect, I recognize that these symptoms were actually <u>warning signals</u> my body was emitting, indicating that something was not quite right (i.e. my internal engine light was flashing). Although at the time, I didn't quite understand the mind-body link as it relates to chronic stress, I was aware that that the way I was feeling was not *normal* and that if I were to remain reactive in my mental state, it would just be a matter of time before these warning signals manifested into something far more serious.

Health Consequences of Chronic Stress

Research indicates that stress is linked to many sicknesses and diseases, and although it may not necessarily *cause* health problems, there is strong scientific evidence that stress is certainly a *contributing* factor.[59] Among the more serious stress-related diseases such as cancer, heart disease and stroke, the authors[60] state that stress is a contributing factor to depression.

To best understand the relationship that exists between chronic stress and depression, we have to revisit an important characteristic of the body's stress response system that was presented earlier in the chapter: you only need to think you are in danger to trigger the stress response. I have learned that depression is a mental disorder that is deeply rooted in how we think and what we believe about ourselves and the world around us.

This is represented by the Weeds of Damaging Beliefs metaphor used in the Deep Well of Depression analogy, which serves to systematically link thoughts-to feelings-to depression. Essentially, how we think determines how we feel, and when we cultivate a system of unhealthy beliefs, we stand to produce a crop of unhealthy emotions (like hopelessness, guilt and so on) linked by the primitive stress response system in the body. This over time can manifest into more serious health conditions, like depression.

The perception of danger, we have learned, activates the stress response. It is not limited to physical threats, but psychological as well. We may perceive that our livelihoods are *threatened* by financial woes, marital problems or guilt-ridden memories from the past. Regardless of the source of these perceived threats, they are filtered the same as if there was an imminent physical danger present. But it is the severity and longevity of a perceived threat that differs in both physical and psychological respects.

That is, the perceived severity of an attacking dog is immediately triggered by our nervous system and processed instinctively through the body's stress response system. As in most acute situations, it does not last very long. However, the perceived severity of a relationship breakdown for example, is consciously determined and influenced by "thinking the worst" in a given situation. We create the threat in our minds and compound it with negative beliefs like *"I'm going to lose everything if we divorce"* or *"My kids are going to hate me"*, all of which activate the stress response.

Unlike acute stress situations, we have learned that chronic stress is characterized as a prolonged stress condition that keeps the stress response system "on", thus preventing the body from returning to a balanced state. As a result, it responds by way of the general adaptation syndrome – that is, trying to function normally when inhibited from returning to homeostasis. It is in this state of prolonged physical and psychological imbalance where we are most vulnerable to treading the Dark Water of Despair.

Healing Requires Balance in Body and Mind

I believe that we must be proactive and responsible in our lives and establish that sense of urgency to do whatever it takes to effectively "turn off" or "turn down" the body's stress response system to achieve, or approach, homeostasis. It is important to acknowledge that the chemical structure of our bodies is not only affected or influenced by *how we think*, but by physical means as well.

STAGE 2: THE SCIENCE BEHIND HOW EXERCISE ALLEVIATES SYMPTOMS

We learned from Stage 1 how chronic stress affects the body and how it can manifest into depression when left unresolved. This section identifies key brain chemicals that influence how we feel (i.e. our mood) and how we respond or act (i.e. our behavior) in relation to depressive symptoms. In addition, this section describes how physical exercise can alter brain metabolism to produce very real physiological changes that can serve as a *proactive* and therapeutic alternative to taking medication for the treatment of depression.

The foremost purpose of this section is to establish convincingly, in the limiting mindset of a person struggling with depression, the importance of recognizing physical exercise as a necessary condition for healing in this disorder.

Four Key Brain Chemicals

Throughout my research on brain chemistry and its relation to depression, I learned about four key neurotransmitters/hormones (i.e. brain chemicals) that influence not only how we feel, but influences how we choose to respond to life's challenges. These include: *endorphins* and a family of chemicals comprised of *dopamine*, *norepinephrine* and *serotonin*.

203

Understanding the complex details associated with how these systems work and function in the brain's biochemical arena is beyond the scope of this book; however, it is essential to understand the connections that exist between these particular chemicals-to both mood disorders and antidepressant treatment. This connection is formally termed "monoamine hypothesis" and is introduced and discussed later in the chapter following a brief description of each of these mood enhancing chemicals.

Endorphins

Endorphins can be described as naturally occurring painkillers in the body that serve to reduce the perception of pain (i.e. acting as a sedative) and can contribute to an elevation in mood.

In one research article[61], the author explains that endorphins interact with opiate receptors in the brain and produces morphine-like properties that reduce the perception of pain and stress in the body, and enhance immune system response. Endorphins are produced and secreted in various ways, such as during excitement and pain, and by prolonged and continuous exercise.

Monoamines

Dopamine, *norepinephrine* and *serotonin* belong to the monoamine class of brain chemicals that influence emotions, mood and behavior. In an effort to draw the connection between these monoamine chemicals and depressive symptoms, I have constructed the following table which links each chemical to their respective mood-affecting functions.

It should be noted that these functions are not exclusive to a particular chemical as they may operate interdependently with one another. The chemical-functional associations displayed in the table, and their relation to depressive symptoms, are compiled from the various sources cited in this chapter.

Monoamine Chemical	Influence on Function: Mood & Behavior	Relation to Depressive Symptoms
Dopamine	Motor activity Attention Memory Motivation (reward-seeking) Pleasure Nausea	Interest deficit Suicidality Psychomotor retardation (agitation) Guilt(worthlessness, hopelessness, regret)
Norepinephrine	Attentiveness Energy Emotion (Stress)	Energy deficit Concentration deficit
Serotonin	Mood Sleep Anxiety Appetite Obsessive/compulsive behavior	Sleep disorder Appetite disorder

Monoamines and mood

Imbalances in these mood-altering chemicals can contribute to a "negative mood" and when left unresolved, can manifest into more serious conditions, like depression.

205

In one article, the author explains how imbalances in each of these monoamine chemicals relate to depressive symptoms: "Norepinephrine may be related to alertness and energy as well as anxiety, attention, and interest in life; [lack of] serotonin to anxiety, obsessions, and compulsions; and dopamine to attention, motivation, pleasure, and reward, as well as interest in life."[62]

Monoamines and behavior

Serotonin and dopamine are known to affect mood, which in turn influences our behavior or decision-making process. In another article, the author states: "...negative moods are associated with negative outcomes"[63]. The same author makes reference to recent studies that indicate that negative emotions were associated with "...increased incidence of depression (and) increased suicide,..." and that "positive emotions protected against these outcomes."[64] The author further states that happiness is positively correlated with serotonin synthesis (or production).

Monoamines and decision making

The brain chemicals dopamine and serotonin serve many important functions in the body. In respect to their influence on mood and behavior, they operate interdependently with one another, and influence the decision-making process.

The author in one research article[65] explains the interdependence between dopamine and serotonin activity, summarized as follows: dopamine is the chemical responsible for the pleasurable feeling you experience when you pursue things that you perceive may be potentially rewarding. Reward seeking behavior then drives the pursuit for gratification.

It is the motivator behind the "wants" and "desires" in life. It could be anything really, such as something as simple as craving a cold glass of water when feeling dehydrated. When you satisfy your craving, it produces dopamine-induced gratification and pleasure. As one can infer, this also applies to the more serious and potentially harmful reward-seeking behaviors associated with drug addiction and alcohol abuse for instance.

The dopamine response is natural and instinctive and is stimulated by what you perceive is rewarding. Furthermore, it does not distinguish between what is *right* or *wrong*, and nor is it regulated by values and morals. So it begs the question then, what prevents us from pursuing our dopamine-influence urges that could result in perceived negative outcomes, like drug use or cheating on a spouse? The answers are *serotonin,* and the last line of defense: *independent will.*

Serotonin Power

The author of the same article describes serotonin as "the molecule of *will power*…"[66] that can "override" dopamine-induced urges or impulses. The author further indicates that "the serotonin system allows you to make the choices you want, rather than have the choices be made for you by circumstance…(and that) proper serotonin activity is necessary to avoid poor life decisions."[67]

One important factor distinguishing both dopamine and serotonin activity with respect to decision-making is that the serotonin system is influenced by values and morals, while the dopamine system is not. In the context of depression, the temptation to turn to drugs or alcohol to alleviate life's pressures, for instance, is a product of the dopamine response. How we actually respond (i.e. our behavior) is influenced by the serotonin response.

When we feel good about ourselves, and our progress with respect to healing in depression, this surge in serotonin activity produces a greater likelihood of making a good life decision, such as choosing not to turn to drugs or alcohol. But unfortunately, when we feel bad about ourselves, and struggle with symptoms like worthlessness and hopelessness, for example, this is associated with low serotonin levels which make it more challenging to resist dopamine-driven urges.

There is however, a saving grace with respect to serotonin imbalance – and that is a single, powerful human endowment called: *independent will.*

Monoamines and Independent Will

We have learned in earlier chapters that the determining factor that separates our emotions from our actions is 'choice'. And how we choose to respond to life's challenges can be influenced by the level of serotonin and dopamine chemicals in our system.

In an article cited above, the author makes the distinction between *free will* and serotonin imbalance: "Low-serotonin activity can lead to impulsivity, aggression, addictive behaviors, and depression. Of course, since you have "free will"…, you can always make the "right" decision, even if it is the difficult one; it's just that serotonin makes it feel more possible."[68]

I believe it is important to acknowledge that as much as this 'chemical imbalance' might influence mood and judgment when having to respond to a particular stimulus, it is precisely that: an *influence*, and not in and of itself, a determining factor.

In other words, regardless of your mood or how you feel, you own the freedom to choose your response in any given set of circumstances by leveraging the human endowment of *independent will*. Recall Covey's explanation of independent will from Chapter 7: human beings have the ability to do what they want to do or what they don't want to do. Or as cited above, "you can always make the "right" decision, even if it is the difficult one; it's just that serotonin makes it feel more possible."

"Monoamine Hypothesis" and Antidepressants

The association between depression and an underactive monoamine system (i.e. *chemical imbalance*) is referred to as the *monoamine hypothesis* and treatment is typically in the form of antidepressant medication. Prozac, Celexa, and Paxil are some common brands of medication prescribed to increase serotonin levels. This in turn affects dopamine and norepinephrine production as these chemicals function interdependently with one another. The result is a chemically-induced boost in mood to create a *feel good* perception.

I have learned in my research that there exists a great deal of controversy surrounding the effectiveness of antidepressant medication and its ability to treat depressive symptoms effectively. In addition, I have also read about the broad range of side effects that can be associated with taking antidepressants, ranging from minor effects like headaches and nausea to more severe effects like suicidal thinking.

Regardless of what one chooses to read or believe about the effectiveness and safety of antidepressant medication, it is a debate that extends beyond the scope of this book. I humbly admit that I do not know enough about this topic to voice an educated opinion, but acknowledge that the term *absolute* does not apply to mental illness. In some cases, treatment using medication may certainly be necessary, and in other cases, not.

This emphasizes the challenge of mental health professionals in trying to determine the best treatment options for persons struggling with symptoms of depression. In one research article, the author makes two important points: "…there is a lack of knowledge on how to best deal with depression and anxiety related symptoms…" and "…the evidence for positive effects of exercise and exercise training on depression and anxiety is growing…"[69]

Making the Case for Exercise to Treat Depression

I stated above that the underlying purpose of this section is to establish *convincingly*, in the limiting mindset of a person struggling with depression, the need to recognize that exercise serves as an effective option to treating depressive symptoms. One convincing factor is that physical activity directly impacts the very same brain chemicals targeted by antidepressant medication. Simply put, physical exercise enhances mood by its direct influence on brain chemistry.

Throughout my research striving to understand the exercise-depression relationship, I found a considerable number of articles and research studies that support the effectiveness of exercise in treating depression:

"Since 1981, more than 70 reviews have been published [on the impact of exercise on negative psychological states] and the vast majority of them…have found that exercise reduces self-reported anxiety and depression."[70]

"A plethora of evidence from animal and human studies indicates that physical exercise improves health, both physically and mentally" and "Regular physical exercise has been proved to have therapeutic benefit, such as treating psychiatric illnesses…"[71]

"More than 1,000 trials have examined the relationship between exercise and depression, and most have demonstrated an inverse relationship between them…Regularly performed exercise is as effective an antidepressant as psychotherapy or pharmaceutical approaches."[72]

"Several studies have found exercise to be an effective treatment for depression…researchers concluded that exercise was…as affective as cognitive therapy in treating depression…In sum, exercise may be as effective as antidepressant medication in the reduction of depressive symptoms."[73]

"The mood benefits of exercise are supported by striking scientific evidence. Exercise can be as powerful as antidepressant medications in treating depression, and, more broadly, regular exercise is linked with decreased anxiety, stress and hostility."[74]

I believe that the message is overwhelmingly clear: physical exercise enhances mood and *can* serve to effectively treat depressive symptoms. I emphasized the word 'can' because I have also discovered in my

211

research an important factor attributing to the effectiveness of exercise in treating symptoms: *exercise intensity*.

One article states that "the stimulation of the monoamine system is dependent on exercise intensity"[75]; in another article, the author states that the increase in motor activity generated by physical exercise is thought to influence the *rate* of serotonin synthesis, and further suggests "aerobic exercise can improve mood"[76]; and in another, the author states that endorphin response increases with exercise intensity and "becomes stronger with exercise frequency."[77]

The Exercise Effect on Monoamine Chemicals

We can take from this research two important messages: firstly, exercise enhances mood by its direct effect on brain metabolism, and secondly, the production and release of these mood enhancing chemicals tend to be correlated with exercise intensity.

In a previously cited article[78], the authors describe the physiological properties that map out how physical activity enhances brain functioning through the regulation of these monoamine brain chemicals. The authors further assert that exercise changes dopamine levels in the central nervous system, enhances stress resistance capability by affecting norepinephrine levels, and increases secretion of the "feel good" chemical serotonin.

Mapping the brain's complex biochemical response to physical exercise extends beyond the scope of this book. However, we can draw a conceptual understanding of *how* exercise affects the brain's feel-good chemicals in relation to chronic stress and depression.

It begins by drawing the connection between physical exercise and the body's natural stress response system that was described in the previous section. Simply stated, exercise itself is a stressor and causes "…a surge of physiological processes (that) floods the body automatically and precisely."[79] In other words, by engaging in intense physical exercise such as jogging, aerobics or weightlifting, the stress response system is activated by the monoamine chemical norepinephrine (among others) which is responsible for increasing heart rate, blood pressure, and redirecting blood flow to muscles.

Another article claims that physical exercise is "…literally one of the most natural means to express the manifestation of the stress response."[80] Exercise causes a boost in norepinephrine by activating the stress response, and according to the table presented earlier in this chapter, higher norepinephrine is associated with higher levels of energy and attentiveness. This is because our body requires more energy to fight or take flight in the stress response scenario, and our awareness is intensified in preparation for the perceived or impending attack. In a different context, engaging in an exercise activity requires higher levels of concentration. It follows then that the exercise-induced boost in norepinephrine serves to counteract the corresponding symptoms of energy and concentration deficits.

There is another important benefit associated with elevated norepinephrine levels by exercise: it enhances stress resistance capability.[81] Alternatively, to reference the American Psychological Association, "…exercise seems to give the body a chance to practice dealing with stress."[82]

213

Exercise Activates the Stress Response

Although engaging in physical exercise does not typically produce a life or death situation, the body instinctively responds to the exercise-induced stress. For example, when we engage in aerobic exercise, certain chemicals and hormones are released in the body by the endocrine system which in turn affects:

...the nervous system, by activation of the stress response;

...the circulatory system, by the increase in cardiac output and blood pressure;

...the respiratory system, by heavier breathing patterns;

...the digestive system, as blood flow becomes diverted to the stimulated muscles;

...the muscular system, by increased muscle tension.

The American Psychological Association further suggests that the exercise-induced workout of the body's physiological systems "may be the true value of exercise" and that "...the more sedentary we get, the less efficient our bodies in responding to stress."[83] It stands to reason that the more physically active we are, the more efficient our bodies become when responding to stress and symptoms of depression.

Exercise Triggers Endorphin Release

Endorphin release is another byproduct of the stress response system when engaged in physical exercise. This, in turn, reduces the perception of pain and stress in the body. Due to its morphine-like properties, the discharge of endorphins contributes to an elevation of mood during and after a workout.

Exercise is known to alter brain metabolism, particularly in its influence on serotonin and dopamine synthesis which we have learned are mood-regulating chemicals. With reference to the earlier table showing chemical-functional associations, serotonin is known to influence a variety of conditions such as mood, sleep, anxiety and appetite. We have learned that serotonin production and discharge is correlated with exercise intensity. When engaging in intensive aerobic activity, serotonin levels elevate, which affects mood, improves sleep patterns, reduces anxiety and influences a healthier appetite, thus helping to counteract symptoms associated with low serotonin levels.

We also learned that serotonin is associated with will power which explains why, in a positive frame of mind, it is easier to make what we perceive are *good* decisions.

Dopamine is known to influence a broad range of functions in the body, but of particular interest are those affected by depressive symptoms, such as motor activity, motivation and pleasure.

In one reference, the author explains that psychomotor retardation is representative of "slow body movements, slow cognitive processing, and slow verbal interaction" and identifies slouched posture, head down, avoidance of eye contact, and simple one or two-word responses to questions, as common characteristics of this particular symptom.[84] Furthermore, another research article explains that psychomotor retardation "…can lead to impaired cognition, judgment, reason, and decision making."[85]

215

The Power of 'Choice' and Exercise

Engaging in intense physical activity requires a conscious acceleration of muscle movement (i.e. increased motor activity) and attentiveness (i.e. coordination of movement). As referenced earlier, the physical demands of intense exercise stimulate the stress response in the body, causing "...a surge of physiological processes (that) floods the body automatically and precisely."[86]

The psychological benefits that revolve around reward-driven behavior are unique characteristics of the dopamine system. This is linked to a sense of fulfillment, or euphoria, when completing an intensive exercise routine, like a marathon for example. This sensation can serve to proactively counter symptoms associated with deficient dopamine production, especially when cultivated consistently. Habitual exercise stimulates and maintains *interest* levels (which serves to counter the symptom of *interest deficit*), and through reward-driven behavior, produces an improved and consistent feeling of *self-worth* (countering the symptom of *worthlessness*) and confidence. In addition, exercise stimulates psychomotor activity by the release of norepinephrine and other steroid hormones, contributing to increased muscle tension, attentiveness and alertness (thus countering *psychomotor retardation*).

Strengthen Mind and Body to Alleviate Symptoms

The evidence supporting the physiological and psychological benefits of exercise, and its therapeutic effectiveness in treating depressive symptoms, is clearly stated. It should also be clear that the purpose of leveraging exercise in this context does not aim to *cure* depression, but rather, to *strengthen* your physical and psychological capacities to enable you to deal with symptoms more effectively (and proactively).

Exercise: The Missing Link

Speaking from personal experience (and supported by a mountain of research), physical exercise is a crucial healing component in depression. Its effectiveness as a healing mechanism strengthens when done on a consistent basis (i.e. leveraging its recurring physical and psychological benefits) and further, research suggests that its effectiveness increases with exercise intensity.

To truly appreciate the power of exercise in managing and countering depressive symptoms, we need to recognize the role physical exercise plays when the body is in a chronic state of stress. Simply, exercise serves as the *missing link* between chronic stress (i.e. when the body is locked in stress response mode) and homeostasis (i.e. when the body is in balance). In other words, physical exercise helps the body to *reduce* the incidence of chronic stress and enables it to, at least, *approach* a state of (physiological and psychological) balance. To illustrate, consider the following stress response sequences that relate to both *acute* and *chronic* stress scenarios:

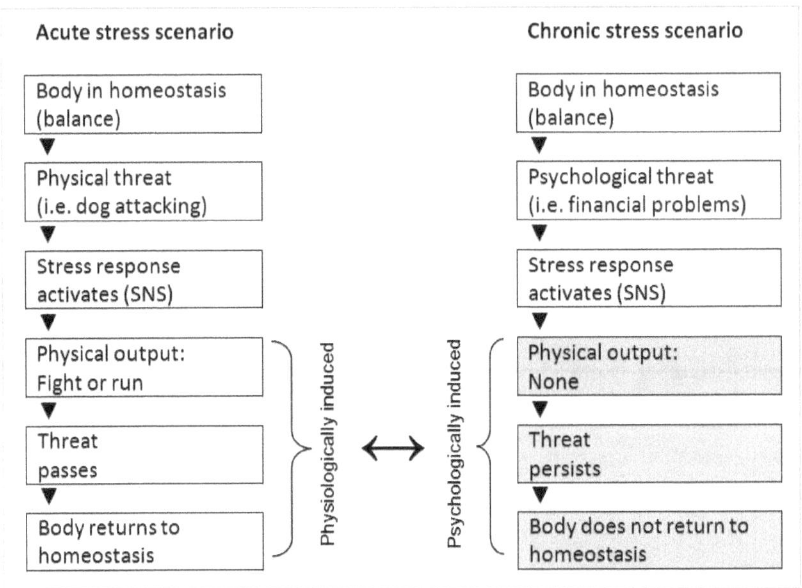

The acute stress scenario on the left-hand side represents the natural sequence of the stress response system that occurs when threatened physically, like being attacked by a dog. Our instincts kick in automatically and the surge of processes that floods the body prepares our physiological systems to either fight or run.

Under the chronic stress scenario shown on the right-hand side of the diagram, the body's stress response kicks in as if a physical threat were imminent. Similar to the acute stress scenario, this results in a surge of physiological processes that prepares the body to fight or take flight even though the perceived threat is psychological and not physical.

In other words, unlike the acute stress scenario, which requires that we expend physical output to fight or run away from an attacking dog, the chronic stress scenario does not require any physical output. In this situation, the body is physically prepared to fight or take flight (i.e. muscles contracted, adrenaline hormones surging, heart pulsating) even though there is nothing to fight or run away from.

It follows then that the *physical output* requirement that exists in acute stress situations is <u>absent</u> in the chronic stress scenario. This is because the severity of a threat (e.g. worrying about financial problems) is measured by how we think about the perceived or actual consequences of the threat (e.g. worrying about bankruptcy). Although there is no dog attacking in the physical sense, your body responds as if there is, like you imagine it happening (or in other words, when contemplating a worst-case scenario). When you can't stop thinking about that imaginary dog, it prevents the body from achieving its desired state of balance. The act of *worry* can persist over an extended period of time, and when left unresolved, can prevent the body from achieving its desired physiological balance. This, we have learned, can manifest into physical symptoms.

The idea behind this perspective of exercise is to <u>inject</u> the chronic stress scenario in the table on the previous page, with a physical element that mirrors the acute scenario on the left side. This provides the body with an appropriate mechanism to expend its survival-induced energy generated by the activation of the stress response system.

When this occurs, a monkey wrench is thrown into the system so to speak. It serves to <u>disrupt</u> the pattern of prolonged chronic stress by introducing to its scenario, a very real physiological and psychological response initiated by exercise. This disruption is illustrated below in the modified <u>chronic</u> stress scenario:

219

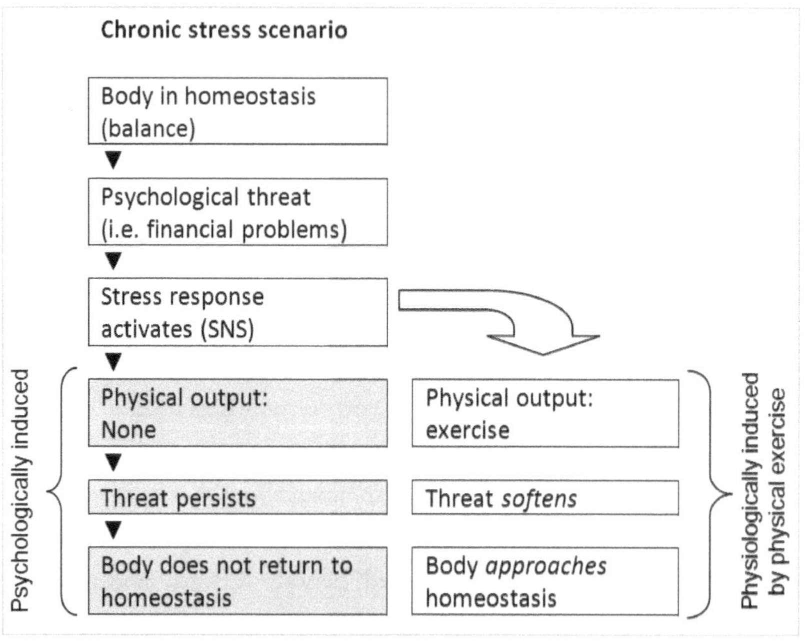

It is important to note that in the chronic stress scenario, exercise on its own will not return the body to homeostasis as there are both physical and psychological elements at play. This is why I stated above that the purpose of exercise is not intended to *cure* depression, but rather, to *strengthen* your ability to deal with symptoms more effectively.

We have learned that by engaging in physical exercise, there are physiological and psychological benefits to counter depressive symptoms. It follows then that exercise can facilitate the body's natural process to at least approach physiological and psychological balance.

STAGE 3: TAKE ACTION AND LEVERAGE YOUR POWER TO CHOOSE

To truly reap the therapeutic benefits of physical exercise when dealing with chronic stress conditions, there must first be a conscious decision to actually engage in exercise. At this point, we know the benefits of exercise, and with this knowledge, we have established every reason why we should adopt a proactive perspective of exercise to help us deal more effectively with symptoms.

Speaking from personal experience, there is a very fine line that separates knowing what we *should* do and making that conscious and proactive decision to actually *do* it. I understand how difficult it is to make the transition from being reactive to being proactive when dealing with oppressive symptoms of depression. I knew that if I were to consciously *choose* to remain footed on a reactive pathway, I would have to acknowledge all that I stood to lose in my life by surrendering to my disorder. As difficult as it was, I had to accept the hard truth that I do have a *choice*. It was *my choice*. Further, I had to accept that no one but me was responsible for the inevitable consequences of doing nothing.

You Own the Power to Choose

If you find yourself in that place where you acknowledge the importance of exercise and desire to be proactive in this respect, but feel anchored in your symptoms, recognize that this internal battle is indicative of chemical imbalance in your brain's metabolism. We now know that low serotonin and dopamine levels can adversely influence reasoning and decision-making skills. Even though we may *feel* stuck in our symptoms,

221

recall that there is one last line of defense we can leverage to help us make proactive life decisions, even when we feel at our worst: *independent will*. This is the time to leverage what Viktor E. Frankl refers to as the *last of the human freedoms*: "to choose one's attitude in any given set of circumstances, to choose one's own way."[87]

Recall the quote introduced earlier in this chapter: "Of course, since you have "free will"…, you can always make the "right" decision, even if it is the difficult one; it's just that serotonin makes it feel more possible."[88] To emphasize: you can always make the *right* decision, even if it is a difficult one.

Proactive perspective of exercise

It is crucial at this time to establish a *proactive perspective of exercise* in spite of oppressive symptoms. Furthermore, this is the time to leverage our human endowments so we can make that conscious and proactive *choice* to engage in exercise. We have learned in Chapter 7 that how we choose to respond to a particular stimulus is influenced by certain endowments and perspectives presented in the Proactive-Liberation Model for Depression:

The Proactive-Liberation Model for Depression

STIMULUS ⟹ FREEDOM TO CHOOSE ⟹ RESPONSE

- Awareness
  - Self
  - Family
  - Third-party
- Shock Emotion
  (Emotional Intelligence)
- Imagination
- Conscience
- Independent Will
  - Motivator Factor

Awareness

In simple terms, the endowment of awareness is essentially opening your eyes and becoming aware of how your condition is affecting you personally, in both physical and psychological respects, as well as others in your life.

With respect to my own personal experience, I woke to the reality that unless I became proactive and began making changes to how I was dealing with my symptoms, my physical health stood to deteriorate. This was a direct consequence of the constant state of emotional and mental stress I was living with day in and day out.

223

Shock Emotion

Following this realization, I leveraged *shock emotion* to separate value-based thoughts from reactive and self-limiting emotions. The conscious ability to extract emotions from your thought process allows you to contemplate objective, well thought out choices to help you respond effectively to life's challenges. I regarded certain emotions like feeling sad or being too tired as nothing more than superficial excuses that served only to prevent me from doing what I felt I needed to do (i.e. exercise) for the betterment of my mental health.

Imagination

With *imagination*, I envisioned myself eventually reaching my breaking point whereby the culminating stresses and overwhelming emotions from symptoms would become too much to bear, both mentally and physically. I could see the very real possibility of experiencing a heart attack, for example, and becoming physically debilitated as a result. I would extend my imaginative exercise by putting myself in my family's shoes (i.e. leveraging *family awareness*) so I could see for myself how my condition was affecting them.

Conscience

By embracing my inner values and listening to my heart, I knew that I had to do what felt *right*, and be proactive in both my mental and physical capacities. I realized that I had to be stronger in body and in mind before I could effectively counter the potentially damaging effects of my symptoms.

Motivator Factor

Whenever I would feel "too bad" to exercise, I leveraged my *motivator factor*. I would think of my little girl and that day when we could go in the backyard and build that snowman together. I knew that if I were physically incapacitated, that day would never come, and I would stand to lose more than a healthy heart. Furthermore, I thought about my kids and became determined to be an example in their lives so that when they get older, they would never perceive their father as a weak, pitiful soul who just gave up on life.

Independent Will

With these personal motivators deeply embedded in my heart, I exercised *independent will* and chose to take action. I committed about an hour each day to some form of intensive exercise to strengthen my physiological and psychological systems. I realized immediately the extraordinary influence exercise had on my mental and physical well-being.

Fully Embrace Your Power of Choice

Based on my own personal experience in this disorder, exercise played a crucial role in my healing process which is why it warrants a single step on the Ladder of Liberation. It was difficult at times to find the strength to exercise in spite of my symptoms, but this speaks to the significance of embracing and leveraging the same endowments Covey speaks to so we can resist the oppressive force of depression and adopt *a proactive perspective of exercise*. I believe that in order to take full advantage of the physiological and psychological benefits that exercise affords, it must be

225

leveraged consistently to build the necessary momentum to drive the healing process.

I further believe that it is important to acknowledge the indirect benefits associated with engaging in exercise when struggling in this disorder: in particular is the support and encouragement from loved ones who see you working hard, trying to help yourself, while knowing it is difficult to do so. Another is the reassurance that your efforts toward healing in this disorder is selfless and dignified because you will ease the pain and suffering of loved ones who hurt because you are hurting - people in your life who adamantly want you to *beat* this thing. By being proactive and responsible in your healing, you demonstrate that you are not surrendering to your condition and that you are going to do everything you can in order to get better. There would be no greater gratification for your loved ones who hurt for you. If you don't see this, then switch places: leverage your imagination right now, think about someone in your life you love unconditionally, and imagine they are suffering with a drug addiction. Think about how that makes you feel. Now think about them fully recovering and being healthy. Did you feel that polar swing in emotion? This is the power of influence your healing has on the well-being of loved ones.

YOUR PURPOSE IS HONORABLE

The most significant benefit one can realize by leveraging our innate human endowments when healing in depression is that your purpose is sincere, honorable and responsible. Choosing to be proactive and exercise is a value-based choice and not a superficial one. That is, you are not choosing to exercise for the purpose of image or because you are influenced by what you perceive others think of you. Rather, you are proactively engaging in exercise because you have adopted that sense of urgency to do whatever it takes to stop the bleeding in your disorder, so to speak. You choose to leverage the power of exercise as a natural remedy to alleviate depressive symptoms. You choose to be proactive and exercise because it will make you better, both mentally and physically. This in turn stands to alleviate the indirect stresses and anxieties that your suffering causes to those who love and care for you. You choose to be proactive and exercise because you are responsible in your disorder.

Ladder of Liberation Step 5: Action Steps to Exercise

1.   *Be consciously aware of how your body is wired*

In order to truly appreciate the therapeutic benefits of physical exercise in treating depressive symptoms, I believe that you first have to appreciate how everything connects together: for example, your thoughts (i.e. perceptions) influence your feelings, bridged by a complex biochemical process. Our feelings (i.e. mood) are regulated by monoamine chemicals. Exercise is known to elevate these mood-enhancing chemicals which in turn, influence positive thinking.

2.   *View exercise as a non-optional task in your daily life*

Read the following quote by Henry David Thoreau: "It is not enough to be industrious (busy); so are the ants. What are you industrious (busy) about?"[89] Ants spend all their time working to ensure their survival: building shelter (i.e. ant hills) and collecting food. Both of these necessary tasks require physical labour. If an ant becomes unhealthy and cannot work, it starves to death. This is the frame of reasoning we must adopt in order to truly embrace a proactive perspective of exercise. That is, we must view physical labour (i.e. exercise) as an essential task to survival in our lives. Consider what I call the *Exercise-Time* paradox: *Life is too busy to exercise - but yet, the quality of life is determined by our physical and mental well-being.* Like the ants, if we are not healthy, we suffer in life. Therefore, engaging in exercise promotes physical and mental well-being – the very foundation that not only supports our quality of life, but improves on it.

3.   *Start doing it!*

At this point, you are consciously aware of how chronic stress and depressive symptoms affect your body. Now it is time to throw that monkey wrench into your system and introduce that missing physical element to your personal chronic stress scenario: exercise. There are two-channels of exercise that corresponds with the "flight or fight" components of the stress response system: aerobic and anaerobic exercise. Aerobic exercise corresponds with the "flight" (i.e. running) component and serves to condition the body's cardiovascular system; and anaerobic (i.e. weightlifting) is related to the "fight" component which serves to condition the muscular system. There are many varieties of aerobic and anaerobic exercise programs available so choose what you feel most comfortable doing. Speaking from my own experience, I took up jogging to condition my cardiovascular (i.e. "flight") system; and weightlifting to condition my muscular (i.e. "fight") system. This is what works for me and I have enjoyed tremendous success in healing by leveraging these types of exercises in my daily life.

A disclaimer on exercise intensity: the primary purpose of engaging in an intense exercise program is to challenge your physical system so you stimulate as much of these mood-enhancing brain chemicals as possible. But it must be done safely. The use of heart monitors are encouraged in order to keep your heart rate within a safe range; and depending on your age and physical condition, it is advisable to consult with your doctor prior to beginning an exercise regimen.

CHAPTER 14

Action Step #6: Embrace Your Positive

The sixth step toward achieving liberation from depressive symptoms requires that we climb out of the Deep Well of Depression. What this means is that by effectively leveraging the underlying principles described in each of the five preceding steps on the Ladder of Liberation (i.e. defibrillating our depression, seeking help, forgiving self, creating purpose, and exercising), we prepare ourselves to *exit* the well.

We are now stronger in our physical and emotional capacities to the point where we can confidently take that next step and pull ourselves up and out of this dark well. We find ourselves then standing next to the opening of the well, exposed fully to the Sun's radiating warmth.

FOCUS ON THE SUN

In Chapter 3, I described the significance of the Sun in this analogy: it represents those things in our lives that we are truly grateful for and are blessed to have. It stands for everything that has true meaning and value in our lives. I also explained that the radiating warmth emanating from the Sun symbolizes the *intensity* of our appreciation for, and the strength of empowerment we receive from, life's blessings. The Sun's rays are felt most intensively at the surface of the well and least intensively at the bottom where one treads the Dark Water of Despair.

In my description on the symbolic significance of the Sun, I explained that when you tread water inside the Deep Well of Depression, the only source of evidence of the Sun's existence (i.e. the good in your life) is a tiny beam of sunlight that stretches down into the depth of the well. In an incapacitated state, the man's perceived inability to consciously lift his head and look toward the tiny beam of light is indicative of a damaged belief system, or what has transgressed into a cesspool of debilitating thoughts and ideals. It is in this mind frame where "irrational" thoughts seep between the cracked crevasses of reality, appearing as though they are "rational," and deceiving cognitive defenses. Trying to convince a person in such a desolate state of mind of all that is great in his life can be a futile exercise because it is something that he must recognize for himself. That is, he must consciously lift his face out of the dark water and look toward that tiny beam of light shining down from the opening

231

of the well. He must *want* to look to it. He must *want* to feel that slight sensation of heat emanating from this tiny beam. This desire to look toward the light is triggered by what was described earlier as a *defibrillator* moment.

My defibrillator experience was surreal, and it served as a powerful call to action. It provided me with that spark – the sense of urgency to do something before it was too late. What I didn't know however, was what that next call to action was to be. My perceived challenges persisted and the Piranhas of Depression continued to thrash aggressively in the water below my feet as I dangled from the first rung on the ladder.

Embrace Hope

My external circumstances hadn't changed but something inside of me did change. My defibrillator experience re-established deep within my heart the single most important attribute that I believe aids in survival when faced with a life threatening situation: *hope.*

Major depression is in part characterized by the neurovegetative symptom of *hopelessness*, or as defined in an earlier chapter, *having no expectation of good or success.* In a hopeless mindset, you fail to appreciate all that is good in your life and your thoughts remain oppressed by a contaminated belief system. In a way, you choose to avoid the sunlight because you have no expectation of anything improving in your life. But with hope, you reclaim that expectation of good or success.

Merriam-Webster Dictionary defines *hope* as: "to desire with expectation of obtainment or to expect with confidence." It is at this point that you desire for things to improve in your life and in the lives of loved ones – believing that by making the resolve to be proactive and responsible in your decision-making, you can confidently produce better outcomes in your life.

This relates to the symbolic significance of the *sunlight* in the deep well perspective healing model: that tiny beam of light, when treading the Dark Water of Despair, provides an energy fueled by *hope*. This serves to strengthen our spirits and motivates us to keep climbing the Ladder of Liberation, no matter how difficult it can be at times. *Hope* is what enables us to pull ourselves up and out of the opening of the well.

Your Defining Moment

This is a defining moment in our healing journey because we are now situated at a place, in the Deep Well of Depression context, where when we look up, we see the Sun and feel its warmth, and when we look down, we observe the dreary abyss of this deep, dark well.

It is at this point in our journey when we begin to see things more clearly: to get here, we learned to adopt healthy perspectives about our disorder, and embraced empowering beliefs that positively influenced our thoughts and feelings. In the deep well analogy, the person climbs out of the well and stands on solid ground. This symbolizes that neutral area in our journey – that sensitive space separating life's challenges from its blessings.

ESTABLISH AND EMBRACE HEALTHY PERSPECTIVES

The key message in this chapter is that when we look toward the Sun in this figurative context, we must learn to embrace healthy perspectives about the things in our lives that we are truly blessed with. Alternatively, when we look down toward the opening of the well, we must be proactive and embrace healthy perspectives about the challenges in our lives – about our Piranhas of Depression.

This exercise will serve to establish a foundation of productive beliefs that can position us to deal more effectively with not only existing challenges, but those we have yet to experience.

This section requires some personal reflection in the context of the Deep Well of Depression. I can leverage the endowment of imagination and see myself standing by the opening of the well. The Sun above me is shining bright and there I am, with both arms extended toward the sky, my eyes closed, meditating in the Sun's radiating warmth. I am closer to the Sun than I was when treading the Dark Water of Despair, and I am standing there taking every advantage to absorb the positive energy that the Sun has to offer. For the first time in a very, very long time, I can fully appreciate the blessings in my life - blessings previously suppressed by a debilitating mental disorder.

Leverage the Power of the Sun

It is critical at this time in the deep well perspective healing model to leverage the radiating power of the Sun. It is time to disempower any recurring thoughts or beliefs that might otherwise cause you to gravitate toward the opening of the well. In other words, this is the point where we must learn to be proactive and leverage our blessings in order to stay grounded at the top of the well, no matter how difficult things may get from time to time. We do this by applying the unweaving process described in Chapter 8 to (neurovegetative) symptoms that shape depression:

1. Sleep disorder (either increased or decreased sleep)
2. Interest deficit (anhedonia)
3. Guilt (worthlessness, hopelessness, regret)
4. Energy deficit
5. Concentration deficit
6. Appetite disorder (either decreased or increased)
7. Psychomotor retardation or agitation
8. Suicidality

The reasoning is that a person who truly feels valued in their life, perhaps by loved ones or society, would likely not be hindered by the symptom of *worthlessness*. Similarly, if a person was hopeful that something positive was going to happen to them – that they had something in their life to look forward to – they likely would not be overwhelmed with *hopelessness*.

If a person was healthy in body and mind, and dedicated an hour each day to physical exercise, then this person would likely not be energy deficient, or have difficulty sleeping or eating, or experience the physical and reflexive slowness associated with *psychomotor retardation*. Rather, they may very well have an extra bounce in their step. In addition, I believe it would be logical to suggest that a person who truly feels content with

235

the blessings in her life would likely not be threatened by *suicidal* compulsions.

The logical argument is that if we are able to establish a foundation of empowering beliefs about ourselves and the blessings that truly exist in our lives, then we can proactively leverage these beliefs to counter or unweave symptoms that collectively shape depression.

Block Depressive symptoms with Empowering Beliefs

The goal at this point in this deep well perspective is to proactively block depressive symptoms with healthy and empowering beliefs. It is important to understand that the effectiveness of this defense strategy is dependent upon our *conviction* about the beliefs that we depend on for protection. Furthermore, our conviction is determined by the degree of *emotional disturbance* from the life experience that underlies a particular belief.

To illustrate, I am going to revisit an incredibly emotional disturbance that I experienced in my disorder: my *defibrillator moment*. Under a contaminated belief system, I was convinced that *my family would be better off without me*. This specific belief cultivated in me the symptom of *worthlessness*.

In Chapter 9, I described my defibrillator experience. I would like to draw your attention to a particular passage that speaks to this emotional disturbance concept:

In my personal battle with major depressive disorder, there was no single rung on that ladder leading up the Deep Well of Depression that produced anything like the mushroom cloud of emotion that erupted inside of me the night I experienced my

236

defibrillator moment. Those simple, innocent words from my daughter detonated in me a shockwave so powerful that it completely demolished the very walls that stood to defend a self-destructive identity that I had adopted and regrettably, hid behind.

My daughter reached out to me that night by asking a seemingly simple question: *When you get better, can you build a snowman with me?* My therapist explained the underlying message of what my daughter was really saying: *Daddy, you are hurting me by being distant and I want you to stop hurting me. I want to spend time with you because I miss you and I value you.* I felt the inherent message in my heart which revealed a new belief that *my family would be better off <u>with</u> me.*

This blatantly contradicted my former belief that *my family would be better off <u>without</u> me* and in turn, this weakened the neurovegetative symptom of *worthlessness* because of my new belief that I was, in fact, valued. This new and conflicting belief grew into a conviction that was so strong it muted the debilitating force associated with the symptom of *worthlessness*. As a result of this single emotional disturbance, the oppressive grip of my disorder eased.

This dynamic can be illustrated using the Depression Severity Range Scale model that I introduced in Chapter 2 (copied on the next page). The feeling of worthlessness was one of the five neurovegetative symptoms that characterized my depression. So it stands to reason in this particular model that by eliminating one such symptom, the severity of my depression then would be reduced to a lower severity along this theoretical depression range scale.

237

This is illustrated by the dot arbitrarily placed at a lower level on the severity range scale reflecting a reduced number of symptoms (i.e. four neurovegetative symptoms) as opposed to five originally (represented by the second dot at a higher level of severity).

Depression Severity Range Scale

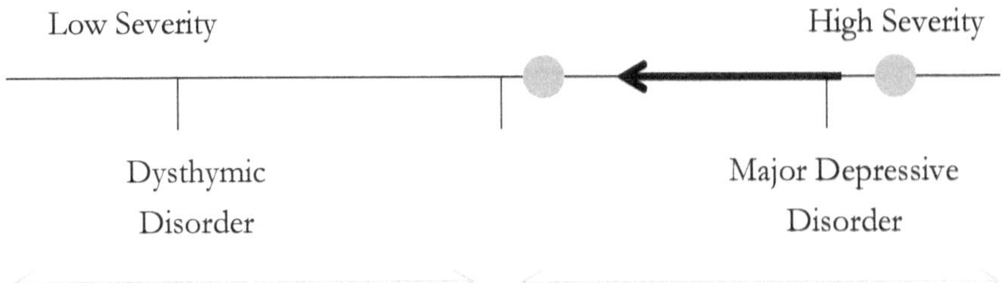

CREATE A CHARTER

The fundamental goal at this point in our healing journey is to embrace, with conviction, healthy and empowering beliefs to disempower oppressive symptoms in depression. We do this by constructing a personal list of convictions – or emotionally driven beliefs that empower us in our journey. I call this list the *Charter of Liberating Convictions* and consider these very convictions indisputable. This list serves as my own set of "Ten Commandments," so to speak, personal *laws* that I depend on to promote and preserve my mental well-being.

Each one of these laws serves to counter a specific symptom of depression, or a combination of symptoms. Once you have constructed your Charter, it is imperative to recite it to yourself daily until it becomes a habit-forming exercise. This will help condition your mind to process the world around you with perceptions grounded on laws specifically designed to empower you in your mental health while, at the same time, disempowering symptoms.

The following represents my own personal laws of conviction from the *Charter of Liberating Convictions* that I depend on daily for my own mental well-being. I am hoping that by sharing my *Charter,* you will feel motivated to draft your own. I recite these convictions every morning so I can start my day with a clear and focused mindset that not just acknowledges my suffering in depression, but more importantly recognizes the valuable lessons that my life has been blessed with as a result of this suffering.

CHARTER OF LIBERATING CONVICTIONS

CONVICTION #1: I am valued.

Statements of conviction: My mental disorder produced in me a belief that *my family would be better off without me.* My daughter reached out to me and showed me that because of my condition, I was hurting her and my family. I now know that I am loved. I know that my children need their father and my wife needs her husband. I know that I need them.

Disempowering symptoms of depression: I am valued and I am loved. Therefore, I choose not to surrender to symptoms of *worthlessness* and *suicidality.*

239

CONVICTION #2: I am better because of my (perceived) mistakes.

Statements of conviction: I have made choices in my life that produced undesirable and sometimes painful consequences. I cannot change my past and recognize that I would not want to even if I could. Who I am today is a product of choices made and consequences experienced throughout my life. Without having suffered, or caused suffering, I would have lost out on invaluable life lessons that consequence affords. These lessons have made me better in so many areas of my life: a better father for my children, a better husband to my wife, and a better person to society. I am able to enrich the lives of others because of my suffering and fully appreciate the honor in my sacrifice.

Disempowering symptoms of depression: I will reconcile the perceived *wrongs* in my life by learning from undesirable consequences and then pay it forward, by being better. Suffering ceases to be suffering the moment it has meaning, and therefore, I choose *not* to surrender to symptoms of *guilt, hopelessness* and *regret.*

CONVICTION #3: I have a purpose in life.

Statements of conviction: I have suffered from depression but in this suffering, I found purpose in my life: to help liberate others from this mental disorder. I have set crystal clear goals that will ensure I accomplish them and fulfill my purpose. I will document my own proactive and responsible approach to healing in depression and will publish it. I will train to be a life coach and specialize in helping people and organizations overcome challenges affected by this disorder. I realize that I will experience challenges in my life that may deter my focus, but I am not afraid. I fully embrace life's challenges because the impending consequences will strengthen who I am and what I will become. I have made the resolve to keep progressing toward fulfilling my purpose.

Disempowering symptoms of depression: I am prepared to suffer, sacrifice and pay whatever price I need to in order to achieve my goals. I promise myself to remain focused and will not allow anything to prevent me from reaching my goals. Therefore, I choose not to surrender to the symptoms of *interest deficit* or *concentration deficit.*

CONVICTION #4: I must be strong in body and mind.

Statements of conviction: My body and my mind are connected by chemical processes. How I treat my body can influence how I *think,* which in turn influences how I *feel.* I will be proactive and engage in intensive physical exercise to stimulate my body's chemistry and leverage this to influence a positive and proactive thinking process in my daily life. From this, I will generate positive emotions and perceptions about myself. I realize that I must work hard to be better physically in order to be better mentally.

Disempowering symptoms of depression: I will leverage exercise to strengthen my physical and psychological capacities to help me process depressive symptoms efficiently, effectively and *proactively.* Therefore, I choose *not* to surrender to symptoms of *sleep disorder, energy deficit,* and *psychomotor retardation (or agitation).*

OPENING OF THE WELL

Revisit the image I described at the beginning of this chapter: *standing next to the opening of the well, exposed to the Sun's radiating warmth.* My eyes are now fixated on the dark opening of the well, the very hole that I crawled out of after successfully climbing the Ladder of Liberation. I am reminded that this was the very hole that I fell through when I surrendered to the debilitating pressures of my symptoms.

Like the previous section where we have learned to establish healthy perspectives about the Sun, we must now focus on the well and establish healthy perspectives about its features, specifically, the symbolic meaning of the Piranhas of Depression.

HEALTHY PERSPECTIVES ABOUT
THE PIRANHAS OF DEPRESSION

When you tread the Dark Water of Despair, or alternatively, struggle with depressive symptoms, it can feel terribly overwhelming. You tend to think about your challenges constantly, which can debilitate a person physically, mentally and spiritually. You see your perceived problems perhaps larger than what they truly are because you are in the deep of it all, smothered by a swarm of these piranhas. However, when we view life's challenges from the surface of the well, you are removed from the painful strikes of each fish, meaning that you no longer feel trapped in your challenges.

From the surface of the well, the Piranhas of Depression appear significantly smaller compared to being in the water with them. This view affords a broader perspective of the overall scope of the challenges you are dealing with. This does not mean they become less important or no longer pose a threat, but rather, it means that when you stand between the Sun and the surface of the well, you are better positioned to process the scope of your challenges in a clearer and healthier state of mind.

You are equipped with that one defining attribute which is otherwise non-existent when positioned in the Dark Water of Despair: *hope*. With a <u>hopeful</u> mindset, you can better acknowledge the scope of your challenges – enabling you to be proactive when having to deal with them. In other words, you choose to learn from the valuable life lessons that emanate from the undesirable consequences that you have experienced. You are hopeful that by learning from your perceived mistakes, you will strive to make *better* choices in order to produce desirable outcomes (i.e. consequences) in your life. When you do this, you will have cultivated a proactive perspective with respect to how to deal with life's challenges when positioned in that place between the Sun and the opening of the well.

Paradigm Shift: Piranhas of 'Inspiration'?

The Piranhas of Depression remain a debilitating threat should you choose to ignore them. In fact, they grow more aggressive the longer your challenges remain unresolved. The implication is that you have a responsibility to them which requires that you adopt a productive and proactive approach to managing your piranhas in this disorder.

One thing for certain is that you cannot escape life's challenges, nor can you shield yourself from inevitable pain and suffering. These are

243

natural human emotions that we all experience. However, we have learned throughout our journey in healing that you do *own* control over how you perceive life's challenges, and, most importantly, how you choose to respond to them. Figuratively speaking, you own the freedom to choose how you will feed and care for each piranha of depression. I believe that when you choose to manage life's challenges proactively and responsibly, the Piranhas of Depression then become less aggressive and more manageable.

This leads to a change in thinking, a paradigm shift, if you will. My perception of these fish has changed and I no longer view them as "Piranhas of Depression," but rather, as "Piranhas of *Inspiration*." In fact, I have come to the realization upon healing in my disorder that the piranhas were never there to consume me as I had once perceived – characterized by their unrelenting behavior. Rather, they were there to *warn* me that certain areas of my life were faltering and required immediate attention.

I have since learned that the more I would ignore the warning signs, the more intense the signals became, or the more aggressive and painful the piranhas' strikes while treading the Dark Water of Despair.

As we are now positioned between the Sun and the opening of the well, I believe that we must be even more proactive and responsible in our thinking by adopting empowering perspectives about each of the *piranha of inspiration*. This provides the necessary momentum as we strive for peace and tranquility in our mental being. It is important at this time to embrace hope and believe that no matter how difficult things might get, our lives can be greatly enriched by our efforts to reconcile those life areas that may be faltering. Figuratively, we can improve our mental wellness by working toward taming the piranhas' aggressive behavior.

POWER OF RECONCILIATION AND HEALING

I believe it is critical to understand and accept that in this productive approach to reconciling our perceived challenges, suffering will be an inevitable consequence. The intransient verb to *suffer* is defined by Merriam-Webster dictionary as "to endure…pain or distress; and to sustain loss or damage." Regardless of the life challenges that you may be struggling with right now, it is essential to believe that in suffering, there is opportunity for growth, but only if we choose to embrace it.

By accepting full responsibility of the choices that we have made, and the resulting consequences that we have endured, we will in time realize through suffering (through pain and loss) that there is opportunity to grow and become better. When we experience suffering in this reconciliation process, we must be proactive in our efforts to alleviate the consequential pain by searching for, and discovering, meaning in such suffering. I believe that when we accomplish this, we are prepared to establish deep in our hearts an emotionally-driven resolve to make the necessary changes in our lives. These changes, when supported by a foundation of proactive and empowering beliefs, serve to enrich not only your life, but the lives of others.

To reference again the inspiring words of Viktor E. Frankl: "For what then matters is to bear witness to the uniquely human potential at its best, which is to transform a personal tragedy into a triumph, to turn one's predicament into a human achievement…In some way, suffering ceases to be suffering at the moment it finds a meaning, such as the meaning of a sacrifice."[90]

In Chapter 4, I shared some insight into my own experience in the context of the Deep Well of Depression. Specifically, about the most vicious of my piranhas: the *Family/home piranha*. Positioned between the Sun and the opening of the well, I can sense some calmness down deep in the Dark Water of Despair.

Calming My Family/Home Piranha

I paid a price for achieving liberation from my disorder. I have the rest of my life to regret losing out what could have been a fruitful, and an unconditionally loving relationship with my late father. At this crossroad, I could spend the rest of my life regretting being bitter and distant. Though I can find some reprieve in the fact that I was a victim of a serious mental disorder, I do hurt when I reflect on what I lost in my life, and am especially disturbed by what I was *about* to lose with respect to my wife and my children.

However, I did in fact discover meaning in my suffering. I recognized that I was afforded the opportunity to learn and be better because of my painful experiences. This has enabled me to *want to* reconcile strained relationships that currently exist in my life. This has encouraged me to *want to* be better in my marriage, and better as a father to my children, especially when reminded about what I lost out with my own father. This serves as the *meaning* of my suffering or *the meaning of my sacrifice*. I now understand in my heart that my father did not die in vain, and as a result, I don't have to allow my regret to torment me. Instead, his death created a noble purpose in my life: *I will be better because of him.* This, I have learned, is the true meaning of a sacrifice.

Ladder of Liberation Step 6: Action Steps to Empower Self

1. Create your very own Charter of Liberating Convictions

The purpose of creating a Charter is to declare with conviction, statements that serve to contradict any limiting beliefs that afflict your mental well-being. These are the statements that when recited every day, establishes a foundation of proactive beliefs that strengthens you while disempowering depressive symptoms. The statements you establish in your Charter must be written in stone, so to speak, supported by irrefutable facts or experiences. Under no circumstances could you ever stand to question or doubt the validity of those statements, even in the darkest of times. By creating such resolve, you will establish a proactive perspective with respect to your challenges. This will enable you to recognize when symptoms intensify so you can quickly calm them with a foundation of proactive and responsible beliefs. For example, when things get dark, and my mental defenses weaken, I will hear the faint, but defeated voice of what was once my Master insisting: *My family is better off without me.* I immediately recognize that this belief is false because it blatantly contradicts Conviction #1 of my Charter: *I am valued* and this belief is supported by an emotionally powerful experience (i.e. my defibrillator moment) that is grounded deep in my heart and could never be challenged. Therefore, I immediately disempower the belief *I am not valued*, a residual belief of the symptom of *worthlessness*.

2. Change your perception about the piranhas: from 'depression' to 'inspiration'

By leveraging the tools learned in this book, this is the time where we face the aggressive nature of each fish-not with fear, but with respect. The aggression of each piranha is representative of the intensity of the warning signals emanating from life's challenges. The piranhas serve to inspire us to be proactive and to make choices that produce desirable consequences in our lives. For example, if your challenge is financial in nature, a proactive choice is to consult with a financial planner; or if your challenge has to do with a marriage breakdown, a proactive choice might be to consult a marriage counselor. Depending on the circumstances, things in your life may become more difficult before they get better. Regardless of what you must endure at the present time, you must believe that because you are being proactive and working to make things better, you will learn in time to appreciate the life lessons that these experiences can enrich you with.

3. *Discover your sacrifice: find meaning in your suffering*

The most proactive and responsible approach to easing suffering is to find meaning in it. When you demonstrate that you are better because of the suffering you have endured, then you are no longer shackled in this disorder. Although you may bear the scars of suffering, they are your battle scars-there to remind you that because you've suffered, your life has been enriched. This is your noble sacrifice.

CHAPTER 15

Action Step #7: Be a Difference Maker

The seventh and final step toward achieving liberation from depressive symptoms requires that we reach out and grip the Rope of Support in the Deep Well of Depression model. Note in this symbolic context that we end our journey the same way that we began it: *by gripping on to the rope.*

Recall that the first step in our healing process required us to leverage our defibrillator experience and reach for the Rope of Support which we depend on to pull us up to the first rung on the Ladder of Liberation. Now, we finish our healing process by reaching again for the rope, but this time at the opposite end, on top of the well. In this symbolic context, we prepare ourselves to pull onto the rope when someone else is in need for support.

However, in the literal context, the logic is not so obvious, and the variables not so clearly defined. I believe that in order to truly achieve liberation from symptoms of depression, we must position ourselves to become difference makers in the lives of others, or someone, or something else. But how do we accomplish this in real life?

The answer is not so obvious because of the gray matter that shrouds this mental disorder. It is not as simple as taking an X-ray to pinpoint the answer. Instead, it requires some digging because lying under this gray matter is the answer you are looking for, and I assure you, it is waiting to be discovered. I know this because we touched on it in Chapter 11 on forgiving self: it is to be the sacrifice for the betterment of another. It is in this moment, when you have truly given a piece of yourself for the betterment of another life, that you will have overcome oppression in this disorder.

I believe that the first step in giving back and being a difference maker in life draws from the lessons learned in Chapter 12 about creating a future goal. The task of creating or defining a future goal to aspire to is a personal exercise, one that requires you to leverage certain human endowments, like awareness and conscience, from the Proactive Liberation Model for Depression. This exercise requires a deep level of soul searching, and listening to the heart.

251

I believe it is equally important to leverage *imagination* in this exercise so you can project yourself into the future along the Timeline of Life Model. This enables you to envision yourself being at that very place in the future where you are presently striving to be. This is the place where you will have accomplished your goal. The next section provides a brief illustration of how I discovered my goal, the attributes I leveraged to achieve it, and how I acted on my goal to become a difference maker in the lives of others.

DISCOVERING MY GOAL

I discovered in healing my said purpose: *I wanted to help liberate others from depressive symptoms.* The question that I had to contemplate next was *how was I going to achieve this?* Before I could answer this question, I needed to take an inventory of my strengths and passions.

Write down things you love to do

I had to take an inventory of things that I truly loved to do – things that I derived great pleasure and enjoyment from. Below is a sample list:

- Communicating with people (having rational and logical discussions, sharing perspectives);
- Creative writing (stories, poetry and lyrics)
- Writing music (playing guitar, writing songs)
- Public speaking (speaking in front of crowds)

Project yourself to where you want to be

Next, I leveraged the human endowment of *imagination*, so I could see clearly in my mind how I could leverage the things I loved doing in order to reach my goal. I envisioned myself speaking in front of crowds, sharing my own personal experiences having lived with this disorder, and the steps that I took to achieve liberation from its symptoms. I saw all of this in my present reality, so the next stage was to take action and make it a reality.

Create your "soap box"

I realized that if I wanted to become a professional speaker on such a difficult topic like depression, a disorder that affects so many people, I needed a soap box to stand on, so to speak. I began by organizing my thoughts and began documenting my research, perspectives and personal experiences, in the form of a book. I wrote about my perception of depression, in the context of a deep, dark well and began to connect the proverbial dots. I wrote as though after having crawled out of the well, I allowed myself to descend back down in order to gain a better understanding of the environment in which I was incapacitated. I used this exercise to gain an appreciation for what I was going through and documented my climb out of this dark place. I wrote as though I was talking directly to the person who would eventually read it, aiming to deliver perspectives that are relatable, practical and simple.

Leverage things that inspire

Next, my defibrillator experience provided me with tremendous inspiration for a song, and when not writing my book, I wrote music. When I completed my song, entitled *"Snowman"*, I felt a sense of accomplishment and was proud for writing something that, to me, was the most beautiful thing in the world. It was an incredibly personal and emotional song and I would spend countless hours practicing, playing and singing to get it to where I felt it should be. This song, dedicated to my little girl, provides me with an enormous sense of empowerment every time I play it.

Find a mentor to guide you

By exercising *proactive association*, I got into contact with a professional speaker whom I had heard about through a co-worker of mine. I admired this person's story and could relate to where he came from with respect to his own personal journey. I told him about my story with depression, as well as my life-changing defibrillator moment, and he was touched by this. In turn, he expressed great interest in helping me reach my goal.

He recognized that there is a tremendous opportunity in this field (i.e. depression) because it is something that affects everyone, but is something that is difficult to talk about. As a result, he agreed to mentor me along my journey toward a career in professional speaking. Through the power of *proactive association,* my contact and mentor helped me on my journey to get to where I yearned to be, a destination he had already reached. This demonstrates the power in proactive association.

THE KEY TO HEALING IN DEPRESSION

This is a personal example of setting a goal and giving back – that is, becoming a difference maker in life. This approach takes into consideration the proactive 180 degree refocus concept from Chapter 12, in which a future goal was defined and the journey towards achieving it was put into motion.

This final step in achieving liberation from symptoms of depression is about discovering purpose in your life. It is about being responsible and proactive, and taking action. It is about becoming a sacrifice for the betterment of another life. It is about self-discovery and embracing your self-worth which, in my view, is the ultimate repellent to any recurring symptom of depression.

I believe that when you have truly given a piece of yourself for the betterment of another, you will have unlocked the key to achieving enduring liberation from depressive symptoms. I understand this is a bold declaration to make, but it is an end result of the very difficult healing process that I have personally endured in my life. This is a healing process based on principles of liberation and survival, and an approach that is proactive and responsible.

Conclusion…

If you are currently struggling in this disorder, or alternatively, if you think you are treading the Dark Water of Despair, I want you to realize that this book you are holding in your hands symbolizes me holding your Rope of Support. I am currently positioned on top of the well with your supporters, rope gripped tightly in hand, prepared to pull you up to the first rung on the Ladder of Liberation. However, it is critical to realize in this moment that you are required to make a conscious choice: you either reach for the rope and hold on to it with all of your strength, or you don't, and you continue to tread the dark water in the depths of your illness.

If you feel trapped in that dark place, overwhelmed by your symptoms, find strength in that tiny beam of light stretching down from the surface of your Deep Well of Depression. Focus on it. Reach out to your loved ones and listen intently to what they say to you and allow them to ignite your powerful defibrillator moment. Hold on tight to the rope and let us – your supporters – lift you to that first rung on the ladder.

Acknowledge that the pain you are experiencing at this moment is paying the price for a better tomorrow: "In some way, suffering ceases to be suffering at the moment it finds a meaning, such as the meaning of a sacrifice."[91] *When* you find meaning in your suffering, I believe you are destined to discover your purpose in life. You will have become the sacrifice for the betterment of others, for those you love. When you truly realize and accept this truth, your suffering will cease to be suffering. When you make your sacrifice, you will hold in your possession the key to achieving enduring liberation from oppression in this disorder.

For years, I have struggled with depression. And in the thirteen months of counselling, the nearly three years of writing and researching, and leveraging the principles of survival and liberation that I was fortunate to have discovered, I learned to successfully overcome each debilitating symptom that once confined me to my Deep Well of Depression.

In closing, be assured that you already possess that single most powerful element to your healing and long-term mental well-being. It is called the *last of the human freedoms* and it is up to you to leverage this as you strive to heal in your depression and overcome its debilitating symptoms:

257

"Between stimulus and response there is a space. In that space is our power to choose our response. In our response lies our growth and our freedom."[92]

I wish you all the best in your mental health.

Jamie Dooks

REFERENCES

[1] Frankl, Viktor E. (2006). *Man's Search for Meaning.* Beacon Press.

[2] Canadian Mental Health Association. Retrieved June 2012, from https://cmha.ca

[3] Mental Health America. Retrieved from http://www.mentalhealthamerica.net

[4] Carlat, Daniel J. (1998) The Psychiatric Review of Symptoms: A Screening Tool for Family Physicians. *American Family Physician Journal, Nov 1; 58(7), 1617-1624.*

[5] Ibid.

[6] Ibid.

[7] Rapaport, Mark Hyman. et al. (2002) A Descriptive Analysis of Minor Depression. *American Journal of Psychiatry, Apr; 159(4), 637-43.*

[8] Meyer, Paul J. (2007). *Become the Coach You Were Meant To Be: The 5 Goals of Leadership.* Paul J. Meyer Resources (Executive Books).

[9] Weisbrode, Kenneth. (2012). *On Ambivalence: The Problems and Pleasures of Having It Both Ways.* The MIT Press.

[10] Unknown author. Quote summarized by Stephen Covey in his book: Covey, Stephen R. (2004). *The 7 Habits of Highly Effective People: Powerful Lessons in Personal Change.* Free Press.

[11] Frankl, Viktor E. (2006). *Man's Search for Meaning.* Beacon Press.

[12] Ibid.

[13] Unknown author. Quote summarized by Stephen Covey in his book: Covey, Stephen R. (2004). *The 7 Habits of Highly Effective People: Powerful Lessons in Personal Change.* Free Press.

[14] Frankl, Viktor E. (2006). *Man's Search for Meaning.* Beacon Press.

[15] Ibid.

[16] Ibid.

[17] Ibid.

[18] Ibid.

[19] Ibid.

[20] Ibid.

[21] Ibid.

[22] Ibid.

[23] Ibid.

[24] Ibid.

[25] Covey, Stephen R. (2004). *The 7 Habits of Highly Effective People: Powerful Lessons in*

Personal Change. Free Press.

[26] Frankl, Viktor E. (2006). *Man's Search for Meaning.* Beacon Press.

[27] Covey, Stephen R. (2004). *The 7 Habits of Highly Effective People: Powerful Lessons in Personal Change.* Free Press.

[28] Ibid.

[29] Ibid.

[30] Ibid.

[31] Ibid.

[32] Ibid.

[33] Frankl, Viktor E. (2006). *Man's Search for Meaning.* Beacon Press.

[34] Ibid.

[35] Covey, Stephen R. (2004). *The 7 Habits of Highly Effective People: Powerful Lessons in Personal Change.* Free Press.

[36] Frankl, Viktor E. (1977). *The Unconscious God: Psychotherapy and Theology.* Pocket Books.

[37] Covey, Stephen R. (2004). *The 7 Habits of Highly Effective People: Powerful Lessons in Personal Change.* Free Press.

[38] Ibid.

[39] Ibid.

[40] Robbins, Anthony. (1992). *Awaken the Giant Within: How to Take Immediate Control of your Mental, Emotional, Physical and Financial Destiny.* Free Press.

[41] Covey, Stephen R. (2004). *The 7 Habits of Highly Effective People: Powerful Lessons in Personal Change.* Free Press.

[42] Ibid.

[43] Frankl, Viktor E. (2006). *Man's Search for Meaning.* Beacon Press.

[44] Ibid.

[45] *Understanding Depression;* (n.d.). A Harvard Medical School Special Health Report. Retrieved from https://www.health.harvard.edu

[46] Olpin, Michael., Hesson, Margie. (2012). *Stress Management for Life: A Research-Based Experimental Approach.* Wadsworth Publishing.

[47] Ibid.

[48] Ibid.

[49] Ibid.

[50] Ibid.

[51] Ibid.

[52] Ibid.

[53] Ibid.

[54] Ibid.

[55] Ibid.

[56] Ibid.

[57] Ibid.

[58] Ibid.

[59] Ibid.

[60] Ibid.

[61] Stoppler, Melissa Conrad. (n.d.). *Endorphins: Natural Pain and Stress Fighters.* Retrieved from http://www.MedicineNet.com

[62] Nutt, DJ. (2008) Relationship of neurotransmitters to the symptoms of major depressive disorder. *The Journal of Clinical Psychiatry, 69 Suppl E1: 4-7.*

[63] Young, Simon N. (2007) How to Increase Serotonin in the Human Brain without Drugs. *Journal of Psychiatry & Neuroscience, Nov; 32(6), 394-399.*

[64] Ibid.

[65] Korb, Alex. (October 2011). *Marshmallows and Monoamines: The neurochemistry of willpower.* Retrieved from https://www.psychologytoday.com

[66] Ibid.

[67] Ibid.

[68] Ibid.

[69] Ströhle. (2009). Physical activity, exercise, depression and anxiety disorders. *Journal of Neural Transmission, June; 116(6), 777-784.*

[70] Reed, Justy., Ones, Deniz S. (2006). The effect of acute aerobic exercise on positive activated affect: A meta-analysis. *Psychology of Sport and Exercise, September; 7(5), 477-514.*

[71] Lin, Tzu-Wei., Kuo, Yu-Min. (2013). Exercise Benefits Brain Function: The Monoamine Connection. *Brain Sciences, January; 3(1), 39-53.*

[72] Schneider, Craig. Wissink, Theodore. (2007). *Integrative Medicine* (Rakel, David. 2nd ed.). Chapter 5.

[73] Ehrman, Jonathan K., et al. (2009). *Clinical Exercise Physiology.* Human Kinetics, Inc.

[74] Otto, Michael W., Smits, Jasper A.J. (2011). *Exercise for Mood and Anxiety Proven Strategies for Overcoming Depression and Enhancing Well-Being.* Oxford University Press.

[75] Lin, Tzu-Wei., Kuo, Yu-Min. (2013). Exercise Benefits Brain Function: The Monoamine Connection. *Brain Sciences, January; 3(1), 39-53.*

[76] Young, Simon N. (2007) How to Increase Serotonin in the Human Brain without

261

Drugs. *Journal of Psychiatry & Neuroscience, Nov; 32(6), 394-399.*

[77] Dorotik, Claire. (n.d.). *Exercise and Mood.* Retrieved from http://www.clairedorotik.com

[78] Lin, Tzu-Wei., Kuo, Yu-Min. (2013). Exercise Benefits Brain Function: The Monoamine Connection. *Brain Sciences, January; 3(1), 39-53.*

[79] Olpin, Michael., Hesson, Margie. (2012). *Stress Management for Life: A Research-Based Experimental Approach.* Wadsworth Publishing.

[80] Seaward, Brian Luke. (2011). *Managing Stress: Principles and Strategies for Health and Well-being.* Jones & Bartlett Learning.

[81] Lin, Tzu-Wei., Kuo, Yu-Min. (2013). Exercise Benefits Brain Function: The Monoamine Connection. *Brain Sciences, January; 3(1), 39-53.*

[82] American Psychological Association. (n.d.). *Exercise fuels the brain's stress buffers.* Retrieved from http://www.apa.org

[83] Ibid.

[84] Videbeck, Sheila L. (2011). *Psychiatric-Mental Health Nursing* (5th ed.). Wolters Kluwer|Lippincott Williams & Wilkins.

[85] *Signs and Symptoms of Depression.* (2015). Retrieved from http://www.healthcommunities.com

[86] Olpin, Michael., Hesson, Margie. (2012). *Stress Management for Life: A Research-Based Experimental Approach.* Wadsworth Publishing.

[87] Frankl, Viktor E. (2006). *Man's Search for Meaning.* Beacon Press.

[88] Korb, Alex. (November 2011). *Boosting Your Serotonin Activity.* Retrieved from https://www.psychologytoday.com

[89] Thoreau, Henry David (16 November 1857). *Letter to Harrison Blake.* Retrieved from https://en.wikiquote.org

[90] Frankl, Viktor E. (2006). *Man's Search for Meaning.* Beacon Press.

[91] Ibid.

[92] Unknown author. Quote summarized by Stephen Covey in: Covey, Stephen R. (2004). *The 7 Habits of Highly Effective People: Powerful Lessons in Personal Change.* Free Press.